I Just Wasn't Made for These Times

I Just Wasn't Made for These Times

Brian Wilson and the Making of Pet Sounds

Charles L. Granata

Published by Unanimous Ltd
12 The Ivories, 6–8 Northampton Street, London N1 2HY

Copyright © 2003 Unanimous Ltd
Text copyright © 2003 Charles L. Granata

A CIP catalogue record for this book is available from the British Library.

Series editor: Leanne Bryan

ISBN: 1 903318 57 2

Printed in Great Britain by Butler & Tanner Ltd, Frome and London

1 2 3 4 5 6 7 8 9

Picture credits

Picture section pages 1; 4 top left, top right, and bottom; 5 top and bottom; 6 top left, top right, and bottom; 7: Courtesy of Capitol Records Photo Archives/Geoff Gans Collection. 2 top: © Hulton Archive/Getty Images; bottom: © Pictorial Press. 3 top: © Michael Ochs Archives/Redferns; bottom: © Pictorial Press. 8 © Richard Young/Rex Features.

Text credits

p. 207 Extracts from *Cheetah* magazine by Jules Siegel. Copyright © 1967 by Jules Siegel. Used by permission. All rights reserved. Mail: Apdo 1764, Cancun, Q. Roo 77501
E-Mail: jules_siegel@cafecancun.com

Song credits appear on page 256

Note: Every effort has been made to contact copyright holders; the editor would be pleased to hear from any copyright holders not acknowledged above.

contents

Dedication

For Kate and Reggie, Jr.,
whose music warms my heart.

To the memory of
Bryce Uibelhoer (1987–2002), and Timothy White (1952–2002).

foreword
by tony asher

I FIND MYSELF, MORE THAN thirty-five years after *Pet Sounds* was first released, with more questions about that extraordinary collection of musical compositions than answers. Soon after its release, it seemed that there would only ever be one seminal question about the album: why didn't it meet with greater success, at least here in the United States, where the Beach Boys' popularity was at its peak? The fact is that, at the time, it seemed clear that *Pet Sounds* was destined to fade quietly into ignominy, joining myriad other such delicately crafted projects. More often than not, such albums came from the most talented and successful artists in the business, and they were almost always invested with thousands of hours of creative effort—to say nothing of hopes, dreams, and expectations.

As difficult as the question about *Pet Sounds* seemed, answers came swiftly. There was no lack of theories to explain its disappointing sales performance.

Some said the record label, notorious in the best of circumstances for its paucity of promotional activity, had no faith in the album (in fact, the label did very quickly release competing Beach Boys product, suggesting that it had given up on *Pet Sounds* somewhat prematurely). Others felt that the album just wasn't what Beach Boys fans were expecting—that it failed to reflect what they had grown to love from Brian and the boys. The fans wanted more of the same, and *Pet*

Sounds was anything but that. Still others posited that the album was simply before its time.

For me, the reason for the album's disappointing sales was immaterial. I was crestfallen—I took the failure personally. After all, I was the only new component in the mix. Over the years, Brian had written successfully with a variety of other lyricists, and it seemed clear to me that my work simply hadn't met the mark. The few reviews I read of the album seemed to focus on the sadness and poignancy of the lyrics, doing so in a way that I saw as critical. There were frequent references to the introspective nature of the subject matter, and when that was contrasted with the typical "fun, fun, fun" attitude of the group's prior hits, even I had to admit we might have been guilty of a tactical error—perhaps a strategic one. (At the time, I was largely unaware of the album's impressive critical and commercial success in England.)

Imagine then my surprise when, in the early 1990s, word began to reach me that the album was having something of a rebirth. I was quite convinced, after all, that the whole project was dead and buried, never to be heard from again. Yet, undeniably, there was renewed interest in it.

A major artist would release a cover of one of the songs from the album. An obscure reviewer would declare it a "must listen." A devoted Brian Wilson groupie from some remote sliver of the world would set up a Web site and ask me to provide an exclusive interview. A long-standing rumor that the label intended to make *Pet Sounds* available on CD—given further credence by Gary Trudeau in his brilliantly provocative *Doonesbury* comic strip—ultimately proved true. It was the first in a series of modified Beach Boys album rereleases.

The momentum built, until the thirtieth anniversary of the album's original release. The interest was truly amazing! The release of the commemorative boxed set was delayed several years past the actual anniversary by the sort of legal squabbling that has become synonymous with the Beach Boys, but for me, the postponement oddly served to accentuate the revived worldwide interest in *Pet Sounds*.

The explanation for that revolves around the fact that I became the default spokesman for the album. Brian, after all, has never been particularly comfortable doing interviews. For one thing, he's a person who expresses himself best through his music. Furthermore, he understandably clings tenaciously to his privacy.

I, on the other hand, have made my living with words (first as an advertising copywriter, and later as a lyricist and editorial writer), which makes me comfortable doing interviews. And, because I have seldom had my privacy invaded by the media (and never on the scale that Brian has experienced), I found the attention interesting, stimulating, and flattering.

Amazingly, the several years during which the release of the boxed set was repeatedly postponed didn't affect public interest in the least, and since its release, the public's fascination with *Pet Sounds* has remained steady, and it seems to keep growing and growing.

Watching all of this has been very gratifying. I've become aware of the powerful impact that *Pet Sounds* has had on other artists. I've discovered that, at the very moment that I was lamenting what I believed to be the initial failure of the album, some of the people I admire most in music were being vigorously influenced by it. Perhaps of even more significance, I've encountered dozens and dozens of people—fans, music lovers, artists, composers, and lyricists—who have shared with me the often profound effect the album has had on their lives.

Time and again, people have told me that for years they've wanted to thank Brian and me for "saving my life." I confess that the first time I heard someone say that, I thought it was merely the sort of excess people are sometimes given to when they meet a person they admire. But, as I listened, I realized that what Brian and I had created truly changed people's lives. That was an epiphany of sorts, I can assure you.

Strangers who have endured difficult, often dreadful childhood conditions have told me that the *Pet Sounds* album convinced them that there were other people out there who understood, and who had survived. If it hadn't been for the fact that they could retreat into that album, they tell me, with its convoluted, compelling themes—musical as well as lyrical—they're unsure of how they would have coped with the reality they were living within. What is perhaps most meaningful about all this is the number of *young* fans who have joined the fray.

What I hope I've made clear is that, in the end, I'm just like you, the reader. I'm quite an ordinary person who has had the good fortune to have my life forever changed by Brian Wilson and his music. While my connection to Brian may seem stronger or closer than that of his other fans, I assure you that we're very much the same. We've all been moved by his music. We've all been inspired by it. We all feel the need to thank him so very much for enduring the slings and arrows that his particular lot in life has inflicted upon him. And we especially admire him for having survived it all. For not giving up. For not giving in. For continuing to bring us what only he can bring us.

It's difficult to believe, when all is said and done, that Brian has turned out to be the survivor. Imagine! He's the one who carries on, with his life, his musical legacy, and his character intact. I would never have predicted it. But I, like others, never fully realized his colossal inner strength, his overriding need to create, or his immense desire to express through music what he cannot express any other way.

Thank you, Brian, for the toe tapping and the finger snapping. For the soul searching and the sympathizing. For all the times we simply couldn't get your songs out of our head no matter how hard we tried. For the times we rode along with the top down singing your songs at the top of our lungs. And for the times we lay across our beds in the dark, unable to do anything more than listen. Thanks for having the guts to lay it all on the line with something completely different, and for believing in a young writer you'd barely met.

A sincere thanks goes to Chuck Granata, who had the exquisite wisdom to understand that the real wonder of Brian Wilson is not to be found within the headline-grabbing antics, the legendary lawsuits, or even the classic dysfunctionality of either his private or public families, but simply in his music.

Tony Asher
Los Angeles, California
January, 2003

preface

"I have touch'd the highest point of all my greatness;
And from that full meridian of my glory,
I haste now to my setting: I shall fall
Like a bright exhalation in the evening."
William Shakespeare, King Henry VIII

I discovered *Pet Sounds* the summer I turned fourteen, courtesy of an elderly neighbor whose musty basement became a clubhouse of sorts for my friends and me—a place for us to play pool and escape the heat of New Jersey's sweltering August afternoons. It was there, among a batch of old records left behind by her grown children, that I found several albums that made a lasting impression on my musical development: *Herman's Hermits, Meet the Beatles,* Bob Dylan's *Highway 61 Revisited,* and the Beach Boys' *Pet Sounds.*

Until that day my sole connection to the Beach Boys was my best friend's sister, whom I considered a certified Beach Boys "freak." But the songs on *Pet Sounds* didn't sound like the Beach Boys songs I'd heard emanating from her room, and the promise of further exploration lured me back to the woman's house day after day for weeks on end. Those hot, sequestered afternoons galvanized my love for the Beach Boys, Brian Wilson, and *Pet Sounds.* The album—recorded when I was barely three years old—has remained a musical touchstone throughout my life.

Why, nearly forty years after its creation, are people extolling the virtues of *Pet Sounds?* Why does it continue to draw the attention of younger listeners seeking enlightenment? What is it about the music that compels us to devour in-depth boxed sets, televised tributes, live performances, and numerous writings on the subject?

Pet Sounds is ageless. Its songs speak to us, their melodies striking emotional chords that resonate deeply within our souls. "Carl and I prayed for people, and for love," Brian has said of the project. "Our original idea was to bring an album that would help bring spiritual love to people."

More than a musical statement, *Pet Sounds* is Brian's magnificent breakaway, his cathartic separation from the Beach Boys. By writing from the heart, Brian reduced sadness and elation to their barest essentials. In making his triumphs and tragedies our own, he created an acutely personal opus that ached with vulnerability. Dennis Wilson once explained how his brother's music could move the band to tears. "We would be in the studio, and he'd play us a song, and we'd start singing and crying. It was so great—it was so beautiful. It was like, 'How could this be happening?' We'd say, 'How'd you write that?' There wasn't one person in the group who could come close to Brian's talent."

Brian's talent and hands-on approach were unrivaled. Like film legend Alfred Hitchcock, he was an intuitive artist who interpreted his vision with exacting care. Just as a film director relies on a cinematographer, location, lighting, actors, cameras, and lenses to shape his vision, Brian used the engineers, studios, microphones, musicians, instruments, and voices to define the texture and sound of his music. His thoughtfulness, flexibility, and innate musical sense were rare, and they endeared him to the most jaded professionals.

"The first time I walked into a Brian Wilson session, I thought he was just another dumb kid," says guitarist Jerry Cole. "I had played twelve-string guitar on the Byrds' 'Mr. Tambourine Man,' and I thought this was another 'kid' project. But we'd walk out of Brian's sessions shaking our heads, saying, 'This son of a bitch is either crazy, or he's an absolute genius.' And the latter came to pass. He knew exactly where he was going. All the piano parts, the guitar parts, the bass parts, the drum parts, and the vocal parts—he knew *exactly* how they were going to fit in his Brian Wilson jigsaw puzzle. And they did."

Pet Sounds reflected a major change in American pop music, and brought an unpretentious elegance to rock 'n' roll music. "God Only Knows." "I Just Wasn't Made for These Times." "You Still Believe in Me." Who else was writing substantial songs like these? Bob Dylan, Paul Simon, and a host of other free-form writers poised on the brink of the folk-rock movement were, but, at the time, they were drawing on social and political events for inspiration. Many of their songs posited dissenting, rebellious views that ultimately fostered change.

But Brian's *Pet Sounds* songs were different. They preserved the innocence of youth, speaking eloquently of love gained and love lost and all the emotional nuances in between. The message was personal rather than social, prodding us to analyze and reassess the way we interacted with each other, not how we interacted with the outside world.

While it was daring to voice one's protest in song, it was riskier still to bare your soul to the world, which is why Brian had little competition. In producing *Pet Sounds* he created and filled his own niche, opening the door for innumerable singer-songwriter-producers working in the exploding pop market. To be fair, some producers were already moving in Brian's direction; the most successful, however, took their cues from the Beatles and Bob Dylan.

Early 1965 found Terry Melcher in the Columbia studios recording guitarist Jim (Roger) McGuinn's band, the Byrds. Their first single, a cover of Dylan's "Mr. Tambourine Man," is one of pop music's all-time classics. It skyrocketed to number one on the charts, instantly launching the group's career while propelling Dylan to the top of the international charts and sparking the growing folk-rock genre. Like Brian Wilson, McGuinn viewed life and music with a sacred eye. "In the beginning it's me speaking to God, saying, 'Play a song for me,'" he said of his performance on "Mr. Tambourine Man." "It's a spiritual testimonial. I got this overwhelming feeling of electricity with it. It was such an experience that I couldn't do anything but submit."

As Brian prepared to write and record *Pet Sounds* in November 1965, psychedelic pop producer Curt Boettcher was beginning to work with the Association, a group best known for its songs "Cherish" (1966), "Windy" (1967), and "Never My Love" (1967). Boettcher, too, liked experimenting with unusual instrumental sounds and, like Brian, he preferred to use studio musicians for recordings. "Along Comes Mary" (a 1966 hit from *And Then . . . Along Comes the Association* album) was lauded by conductor Leonard Bernstein as "cutting-edge pop." Like the Byrds, the Association was enamored of Dylan, and they covered his "One Too Many Mornings" on their first single for Valiant Records.

1966 was a pivotal year for music. Dylan's *Blonde on Blonde* was released, as were key albums by the Rolling Stones, the Mamas and the Papas, Simon and Garfunkel, the Rascals, and Donovan. The best-remembered songs of 1966 represent a diverse range of styles and moods: "Winchester Cathedral" (New Vaudeville Band), "Bus Stop" (the Hollies), "Day Tripper" (the Beatles), "These Boots Are Made for Walkin'" (Nancy Sinatra), "I'm a Believer," (the Monkees), "Lightnin' Strikes," (Lou Christie), "Ballad of the Green Berets" (Ssgt. Barry Sadler), "The Pied Piper" (Crispian St. Peters), "Working My Way Back to You" (the Four Seasons), "Cherry, Cherry" (Neil Diamond), "That's Life" (Frank Sinatra), "Summer in the City" (the Lovin' Spoonful), and "You Can't Hurry Love" (the Supremes).

Singles ruled the industry, but *Pet Sounds* helped to force the emergence of the 12-inch, long play album as a viable medium for the rock genre. At the time, few teenaged listeners invested in albums, which were a format that was generally reserved for their parents, who listened to classical music, jazz, or traditional pop artists such as Frank Sinatra. While it produced three hit singles, *Pet Sounds* represented the essence of what a cohesive, long-play rock 'n' roll album should, and could, be.

Although the Beatles would perfect rock's long form with *Sgt. Pepper's Lonely Hearts Club Band* in 1967, Brian's work on *Pet Sounds* helped egg it on. Beatles producer George Martin recently revealed the extent of Brian's effect on the most influential band in rock music history. "It could be argued that the Beatles had become the most important group of the '60s—they defined the era," he said in 2001. "Yet I have to say that Brian was the musician who challenged them most of all. No one made a bigger impact on the Beatles than Brian."

While mid-1960s folk-rock music provides a colorful snapshot of the psychedelic era, much of it sounds dated. Conversely, *Pet Sounds* has retained its freshness and maintains a relevance. Although it didn't speak of peace and war, this watershed creation—written and recorded in relative isolation—was a product of its time, obliquely shaped by the social turmoil that Brian witnessed around him.

The Vietnam War was raging, and two hundred young Americans were being shipped back to the United States each week—in body bags. Race riots were breaking out in Ohio and Georgia. Comedian Lenny Bruce (who died of a drug overdose in August 1966) was pushing the envelope with his hard-edged, sardonic style. And the Supreme Court issued its landmark "Miranda" ruling, which preserved the rights of criminal suspects. The world seemed poised on the brink of disaster, heightening the need for global peace and songs to promote that message. In the midst of the ungodly chaos, *Pet Sounds* arrived.

While Brian's emotional fragility colors the album's tone, there's an equal amount of jubilant optimism etched into its grooves. With these songs, Brian was saying, "Despite the difficulties, everything will work itself out. Things can—and will—get better." It buffered the uncertainty of changing times, and the anxiety over social disarray in America. It was a record to make you feel good. *Pet Sounds* was the answer to a generation's prayer.

"*Pet Sounds* represented a special moment in history," says songwriter Jimmy Webb. "Brian Wilson came together with the technology, the record business was blooming, and the youth culture in America was taking off. Today, people are always wistfully trying to hope another 'lost' Beach Boys album into existence. They're hoping that someone will find a tape, and that it will be this mythical album that Brian made. But it's not necessary, because the album is there. *Pet Sounds* is the album, and it could only have happened exactly the way that it did. It's a confluence of powerful influences, and a manifestation of our culture in sound."

For Brian Wilson and the Beach Boys, *Pet Sounds* marks a beginning and an end. Neither before nor after did either surpass the musical depth attained in these recordings. Brian's energy surged only occasionally after 1966, resulting in brief bursts of musical excellence. But never again would he or his bandmates match the consistently high musical values condensed into the 36 minutes that comprise this seminal recording.

Pet Sounds is much more than a record; it is an emotional experience to be felt, understood, savored, and enjoyed. Long after we're gone, its irrepressible spirit will survive, and its messages of love, hope, and fear will nestle their way into the hearts and souls of a new generation.

early history

"As far back as I can remember,
there's been music in my life."

Brian Wilson

"Without Brian, there wouldn't have been any Beach Boys."

Recording engineer Chuck Britz

Some people would say that the Beach Boys were born on Labor Day weekend, 1961, when three brothers, one cousin, and a friend rented the equipment required to make their first "demo" recording. Others might contend that the group didn't emerge until "Surfin' USA"—their first big hit— entered the number three spot on the *Billboard* charts in 1963. Then again, a convincing argument could be made that the fate of the band was sealed with the birth of Brian Douglas Wilson on Saturday, June 20, 1942.

In reality, it all began with a radio.

"In junior high school Brian would eat dinner, and he'd go into his room and that radio would be on constantly," his mother Audree explained. "I remember [Brian's father] Murry once saying to me, 'Do you think we should worry about him?' I said, 'No. He's just loving the music.'"

Music—and the tiny transistor radio he kept hidden under his pillow at night—became Brian's constant companions, exposing the boy to a wide variety of genres and styles. "My favorite [station] was KFWB in Hollywood," Brian said. "Every record had something you would listen to; every record had some kind of twist in it that gave you that feelin', and you'd say, 'Oh, man.' You'd go to the piano and say, 'Now, how did they do that?' You'd start learning about it—it's an education. Anybody with a good ear is gonna pick up on those records."

Brian's passion delighted his parents, and it was a rare day that Murry—an aspiring songwriter—didn't hammer out his latest creation on the family's piano for Brian's entertainment. For her part, Audree shared her small record collection with her son, beaming when he begged to hear Glenn Miller's big band rendition of "Rhapsody in Blue."

The Wilson Family

In the early 1940s, the Wilsons lived in a small house at 3701 West 119th Street in Hawthorne, California, an inland town off the Pacific coast area known as South Bay. Hawthorne was a blue-collar town, and Murry tried hard to provide a comfortable life for his family, who also benefited from the support of various relatives scattered throughout the area. Brian forged a special relationship with Audree's father, who, until his death in 1948, would take the boy on explorative flights in his single-engine prop plane.

The family was also close to Audree's sister Glee Love, who lived in nearby View Park with her husband Milton and their six children: Michael, Stanley, Stephen, Maureen, Marjorie, and Stephanie.

By the end of 1946, the Wilson family included two more children: Dennis Wilson (born on December 4, 1944) and Carl Wilson (born on December 21, 1946). All three of the Wilson boys were gregarious and athletic, and they engaged in the harmless pranks typical of boys their age. From a distance, the Wilsons appeared to be a happy family who enjoyed the idyllic environs that southern California had to offer. In reality, relations within the family unit were neither healthy nor respectful.

As a father, Murry Wilson was an inscrutable failure. On the surface, he appeared to be a strict disciplinarian who wanted the best for his children. But deep down, he was a ruthless egomaniac whose parenting philosophy was skewed by his own experience as the child of an abusive, alcoholic father. Life in the Wilson house wasn't easy, and each of the boys dealt with the dysfunction in a different way.

Carl, who died of lung cancer at age 51 on February 6, 1998, was the least affected by his father's misdeeds, and emerged as the family mediator.

Dennis, the rebellious middle child, endured the most punishment. As a youngster he was beaten frequently, and he responded to provocation with a quick temper and fists. Throughout his life, Dennis seethed with anger, and the physical confrontations between father and son lasted well into adulthood. Dennis was the first of the brothers to experiment with alcohol and other drugs. After two decades of reckless behavior exacerbated by chronic substance abuse, he drowned on December 28, 1983, in Marina del Rey, California. He was 39.

Brian suffered too. While his wounds were more psychological than physical, Murry didn't refrain from hitting him. One of Brian's most vivid childhood memories is of his father slapping the side of his head—a punishment that he once blamed for the deafness in his right ear.

Music in the Air

To compensate for his lack of emotional intelligence, Murry showered his boys with music: pianos, a Hammond organ for the family room, and lessons all around. When the Four Freshmen performed at the Crescendo, the man who mercilessly belittled his children struggled to find the money to buy tickets so Brian could attend.

Murry was gruff, but listening to and writing music was one of the few things that tempered his coarseness. He was particularly proud when pop arranger Jimmy Haskell recorded two of his songs, "Fiesta Day Polka" and "Hide My Tears" in the early 1950s. Later, the Bachelors recorded his inane "Two-Step Side-Step," which was subsequently featured by Lawrence Welk and his orchestra on a radio program originating from Santa Monica's Aragon Ballroom. But as hard as he tried, his songs were just too schmaltzy for the rapidly evolving pop market, and except for a few tunes issued as 78-rpm singles, Murry's music went unnoticed.

At home, music became Murry's sole emotional connection to his children—a rare gift bestowed with unrestricted love. "I remember that music was always present," Carl told journalist Geoffrey Himes in 1983. "We always had a couple of pianos and a jukebox in the house. We had a garage that my dad fixed up into a den. We'd all get around the piano; my mom would play, and later Brian started to play. By age 10, he was already playing great boogie-woogie piano!"

Brian also sang in the choir at Inglewood Covenant Church, where the director discovered that, even with his hearing loss, the boy had perfect pitch. He blended nicely with the main choir, and his clear soprano voice projected beautifully when he sang solo. While it was apparent that he was the one blessed with an ear for music, Brian encouraged Dennis and Carl to join him in singing hymns. "The three brothers used to harmonize in bed," Brian remembered. "We'd all sleep in the same room. We used to sing this song, 'Come Down, Come Down from the Ivory Tower.' We developed a little blend, which aided us when we started getting into the Beach Boys stuff."

Music became Brian's escape. He mastered and outgrew his child-sized accordion, and when the family budget precluded the purchase of a larger one, he turned to the family piano, spending hours picking out his favorite tunes by ear. He was a good listener with an interest in a wide variety of music; among his favorite artists were Roy Rogers, Carl Perkins, Bill Haley, Elvis Presley, Henry Mancini, and Rosemary Clooney.

Brian's tastes were also genteel; he revered George Gershwin, as well as the cultivated sound of the top male jazz vocal quartet of the day: the Four Freshmen. Like "Rhapsody in Blue," the Freshmen remained a constant favorite of Brian's and they provided the leitmotiv of Brian's musical life.

His interest in the group was obsessive, and no afternoon was complete without a stop at Melody Music or Lishon's Record Store in Hawthorne, where he could sit in a listening booth for hours auditioning Freshmen records. The sessions became Brian's musical primer—the best investment his after-school-job money could buy. "As a 12-year-old, he was heavy into the jazz vocals of the Four Freshmen," Carl Wilson said. "He would listen to their records and play the harmonies on the piano. What he would do is sit at the piano and figure out each part. Then he would teach Mom and me a part. He would sing the third part, record the three of us singing together, and then he would sing to the playback to hear the fourth part."

The Wilson family sing-alongs helped unite the family, which often included the Love clan. "We loved all the songs with falsetto and bass parts," says Mike Love. "Songs like 'Speedo' by the Cadillacs, and 'Hully Gully' by the Olympics were among our favorites. I would sing the bass, Brian the high, and Carl the middle part. Maureen or my Aunt Audree would take up the fourth part. It was always a search to find the person to sing that fourth part with us. It wasn't a formal group at the time—it was just me and Brian getting together at his house or mine."

The formation of the Beach Boys sprang from these impromptu gatherings. The main proponents of the idea were Brian and his high school football teammate Al Jardine. Born in Lima, Ohio on September 3, 1942, Jardine moved to Hawthorne as a youngster, and was the starting fullback on the high school football team. An avid Kingston Trio fan, Jardine sang with the Islanders, a local folk group. He and Brian became friends during the 1957 football season, and they rekindled their friendship at El Camino College in 1960.

Seeking members for their group, Brian and Al turned to Carl Wilson, who, in addition to playing guitar, had a mellifluous vocal tone similar to Brian's. They also invited Mike Love, who had a knack for writing lyrics. At the time, Love—who had recently married—was supporting himself by pumping gas at a local filling station. He was also spending an increasing amount of time fishing at Redondo Beach with his cousin Dennis, who raved about the surfers invading the Manhattan Beach coastline.

Surf's Up

Although Brian hadn't considered including him in the band, Audree intervened, and Dennis—the least musically inclined Wilson brother—was welcomed to the fold. At the time, Brian didn't realize that his brother's all-consuming habit, surfing, would provide a foundation from which the band could spring. As Carl remembered, Dennis's passion inspired the group's identity and their earliest songs. "Dennis was the only real surfer in the group," he explained. "I tried it, but I was never good, so I gave it up. Dennis was really living it—it was his life.

"Brian drew on Dennis's experiences. I remember Brian drilling Dennis on what was going on—really pumping him for the terminology. Dennis was the embodiment of the Beach Boys; he lived what we were singing about. If it hadn't been for Dennis, the group wouldn't have happened in the same way. I mean, we could have gotten it from magazines like everyone else did, but Dennis was out there doing it. He made it true."

The southern California surf scene that attracted Dennis was a fascinating phenomenon; a rare moment in cultural history that affected everything from music and fashion to travel and lexicon. Introduced to the West Coast in 1907 by Irish-Hawaiian surfer George Freeth, the fad exploded in the late 1950s, spilling into every aspect of the Southern California lifestyle.

"Surf culture was a burgeoning Southern California trend that was taking hold in all areas of pop culture: it affected the way people dressed, the vernacular (surf lingo and slang), cars—everything," says 1960s pop culture historian Hal Lifson, author of *Hal Lifson's 1966!* "Music became a big part of that subculture. The Southern California music scene consisted of groups like the Challengers, the Tornadoes, and the Ventures—it wasn't four guys in Brooklyn standing around a garbage can warming their hands over a fire singing doo-wop songs."

Surf music's blistering arrival came in late 1959 via the renegade Dick Dale, better known as the "King of the Surf Guitar." Dale produced a guitar sound unlike any other, and his regional hits "Miserlou" and "Surf Beat" were seminal recordings that helped to establish the genre. For Dale, power was everything: playing live at venues such as the Rendezvous Ballroom on the Balboa peninsula, in Newport Beach, California, he cranked the volume up mercilessly, creating a passionate frenzy among his audience. Under the guitarist's hand, amplifiers burned up and speakers blew out. "The feeling that I was trying to exert through my music was a feeling of vibration and pulsification. I wanted to match the feeling that I had while I was surfing, and I couldn't get that feeling by singing," Dale told surf music expert John Blair. "There was a tremendous amount of power I felt while surfing, and the feeling of power was simply transferred from myself into my guitar when I was playing. I wanted to make the sound harder and more powerful."

The raw punch of Dale's sound wasn't lost on Carl, who strove to emulate his style. Dennis, totally absorbed in the surf scene, enthusiastically shared tales about his surfer friends, the girls on the beach, and the throaty roar of the musical sounds he was hearing on the coastline with big brother Brian.

Dennis's gushing convinced Brian that following the surf craze might be the way to go. He gathered everyone together to work out some original songs. "Sometime in late August 1961, my brothers Carl and Dennis, my cousin Mike, and our friend Al Jardine and I sat in our den trying to write a song about surfing," Brian explained in 1964. "Actually, Mike and I ended up writing the song several days later; it was called 'Surfin'.' We really didn't accomplish much that night, but it was probably the most significant evening in our whole lives—it was the first group gathering of what is now known as the Beach Boys."

The Beach Boys

The band's debut came over the 1961 Labor Day weekend. With Audree and Murry Wilson away on vacation, the boys let loose. Fueled by Dennis's prodding (plus two hundred dollars left by Murry for essentials, and some additional funding from Al's mom, Virginia Jardine), Brian and Al rented the instruments, amplifiers, and microphones needed to record "Surfin'."

For three days the quintet (along with 13-year-old neighbor David Marks) recorded take after take on Brian's reel-to-reel tape recorder. Murry arrived home and exploded upon learning that the boys had squandered the money. But the music worked its magic, and he softened upon hearing the song, sheepishly admitting "they were on to something." To show his support, he arranged for a demo session at the home studio of his music publisher and friend, Hite Morgan of Guild Music.

Using an Ampex 200 tape machine, Morgan recorded "Surfin'," and the boys' rendition of two Morgan family ballads: "Luau" (penned by son Bruce) and "Lavender" (written by wife Dorinda) on September 15, 1961. The instrumentation was sparse, the vocals handled by Brian, Carl, Dennis, Al Jardine, and Mike Love, who sang to Carl's lone acoustic guitar. Pleased with the results, Morgan scheduled additional time at World Pacific Studios in Hollywood. The October 3 session yielded additional takes of "Surfin'" and "Luau." Believing that "Surfin'" could be a hit, Morgan arranged to have it issued as a single on Herb Newman's Candix Records.

The group elected to call themselves the Pendletones, in honor of Dick Dale's Del-Tones and the Pendleton shirts that were popular with the surf crowd. At the last minute, however, a conflict with another band using that name forced a change in the band's name. As a substitute, record distributor Russ Regan came up with "the Beach Boys." "Surfin'" was released on December 8, 1961, and Newman immediately delivered a copy to KFWB radio, where it was quickly voted the station's top single in a listener poll.

Within three weeks, "Surfin'" shot to number 33 on KFWB's "Fabulous Forty" playlist; it stayed there for three months, topping out at number 3. In early 1962 the song emerged in the 118th spot on a list of records bubbling under *Billboard*'s "Hot 100." Then, the last week of January saw *Cashbox* magazine select the platter as the "Hit Pick of the Week." The Beach Boys were stunned. "Dennis was so thrilled, because he was living it," Carl said. "He went to school and his friends said, 'we were on our way home from the beach, totally exhausted from riding the waves all day. We heard your record come on, and it turned us on so much that we went back to the beach!'"

Although it was unpolished, "Surfin'" brought a new twist to surf music, and it became the foundation of the Beach Boys' evolving style: an unusual combination of surf music and the rock 'n' roll, R & B, and doo-wop the boys heard on the radio.

"What we heard on Los Angeles radio when we were 10, 11, and 12 years old was the 'coming of age groove,'" explains Bruce Johnston, who became a Beach Boy on April 9, 1965. "In the late '50s and early '60s, all of the Beach Boys were listening to KFWB, and to KGFJ—an R & B station that was 1,000 watts by day, 250 by night. As kids, we were attracted to the KGFJ groove, and in that groove were all the vocal parts that were so different from anything else we were hearing."

Although "Surfin'" was a local success, the group's relationship with Hite Morgan became strained. By March 1962 their association with Candix and Morgan had ended, causing them to scurry for a new label. To compound their problems, Al Jardine left the group to continue his studies. To take his place, Brian rerecruited David Marks, whose parents had curtailed his involvement with the band shortly after the Labor Day weekend jam session. (Jardine returned one year later, at Murry's urging, and for a time, both Jardine and Marks toured with the group. However, Murry used Jardine's re-entry to help nudge Marks—whom he disliked—out of the band. Marks rejoined the Beach Boys touring band in 1997, but left the next year due to illness.)

With no label affiliation or producer to plug it, the band was losing the momentum that it had gained during the previous six months. In April, Murry—who had appointed himself their manager—ushered the boys into Western Recorders on Sunset Boulevard to improve on two of the Hite Morgan productions. At this session, the Beach Boys recorded "Judy" and remastered "Surfin' Safari"—two songs recorded at earlier sessions. Murry intended to pitch the songs—and the band—to Capitol Records. They also recorded "409," a song written by Brian and hot rod enthusiast Gary Usher. Engineer Chuck Britz was at the control board for the session. "When I first heard them, I said, 'It's totally different,'" he recalled. "I thought, 'Here is something very creative, because it's new—nobody else is doing this.' It was a different type of a sound."

Armed with the Western demos, Murry approached Nik Venet, one of Capitol's youngest producers. Venet was instantly receptive. "Every once in a while as a producer, before the second eight bars have spun around, you know that the record is a number-one record," he said. After shuttling Murry out the door, Venet called senior producer Voyle Gilmore into his office, and the pair listened to "409" without the distraction of Murry's incessant prattling. By the end of the record, both producers knew they were on the brink of musical history. "I wasn't one for hiding my feelings," Venet said. "If I wanted to drive a bargain, I should have just sat there mum. But I got all excited. I started jumpin' around, telling Gilmore, 'We have to make a deal.'"

The offer tendered was conservative: Capitol would purchase the Western demos for three hundred dollars, and pay the group a five percent royalty. Although it involved only a small amount of money, the deal gave the Beach Boys widespread distribution—and the chance to record more of their music in a professional setting.

As producers, Venet and Gilmore had much to gain, knowing that the Beach Boys could put Capitol Records—and California—on the rock 'n' roll map. "It was a shot in the arm for the entire industry," Venet said. "It was a new form of teenage music. It had nothing to do with your girlfriend breaking up [with you], or driving off a cliff. It was a pure California phenomenon. The Beach Boys represented California to the rest of the country."

After signing with Capitol on July 16, 1962, the Beach Boys, Murry Wilson, and Nik Venet planned their entry into the mainstream market. As their first Capitol single ("Surfin' Safari," backed by "409") rose on the charts, the band entered the Capitol Records studios at Hollywood and Vine to record their first album, *Surfin' Safari*.

By then, America was reveling in the bright new sound of the Beach Boys singing glowingly of the California sun, the elation of young love, and the thrill of owning a high-powered hot rod. By the year's end, the band had settled into a comfortable groove, combining raw surf chords, gritty R & B riffs, and the impulsive freshness of early rock 'n' roll into what was quickly becoming their established "sound."

It was Chuck Berry's "Sweet Little 16" that became the melodic base for their first Top 10 hit and their unofficial anthem. "Brian had this idea to change 'Sweet Little 16' into 'Surfin' USA,'" Carl explained. "When we heard 'Surfin USA,' we just knew it was going to be an undeniably big hit. It was the first time we were aware we could make a powerful record. We were total Chuck Berry freaks, and the original Chuck Berry record is a fabulous record. But, we made it our own." The record topped out at an impressive number three on the *Billboard* charts—ample proof that the Beach Boys had arrived.

fresh sounds

"They could sing a cappella
and make tears come to your eyes."

Recording engineer Chuck Britz

"Brian took the sounds that we made and ran with them.
Took them to the beach, and got on a surfboard with 'em.
He developed summery, carefree sounds around the long
tones—a direction we never went in. For us to say that he
copied us would be false; it was his unique sound."

Ross Barbour of the Four Freshmen

By the time they recorded the song "Surfin' USA," the Beach
Boys' silken vocal sound had become the hallmark of their
distinct musical signature. "What is unique about our
sound?" Brian asked in 1965. "Possibly the quality of my
voice, the higher range of our total voices, the different
variations in production techniques, arranging, and, of
course, songwriting."

Although the instrumentals provided a solid foundation
for their music, the most appealing part of the Beach Boys
sound is their crisp, unified blend of vocal harmonies. The
concentrated beauty was no accident: Brian used the vocal
talent at hand in a carefully measured way. "I love the human
voice for its own sake," he explained. "But I can treat it with
some detachment—as another musical instrument. This
doesn't imply a lack of respect, because I respect all
instruments, from Jew's harp to spinet."

The creation of the vocal blend was both musical and technical. "For 'Surfin' USA' we developed a stylish sound," Brian told journalist Earl Leaf in the mid-1960s. "The high sound became *our* sound. It was the first time we had ever sung our voices twice on one record." Vocal doubling was not new in the '60s; other American groups had experimented by overdubbing on four- and eight-track recorders. In England, the Beatles were using ADT (Artificial Double Tracking) to fatten the sound of the harmony on albums including *Rubber Soul* and *Revolver.* But Brian took the concept to the outer limits of recording technology, and it had a tremendous effect on the sound of their vocals.

More intriguing is the way Brian wove some obvious (and some not so obvious) influences into the vocal blend: nestled inside the nooks and crannies of their homogenized style are strains of jazz, folk, barbershop harmony, and old-fashioned street-corner doo-wop. Combining these diverse styles to attain a fresh vocal sound was shrewd; in doing so, the Beach Boys spawned a new sub-genre of rock 'n' roll music.

The Vocal Influence

Like most harmony groups, the Beach Boys believed that excess instrumentation detracted from their vocal purity, and in keeping with doo-wop style, vocals remained their focus. Traces of doo-wop can be heard in their music as early as their first recording session. "The doo-wop influence came from Mike Love," says Bruce Johnston. "When Brian taught us our vocal parts, Mike would simply join in with an improvised bass part, aiming for the 'figured bass groove' prevalent in the Coasters' music."

The traditional '50s doo-wop style takes on a new dimension when juxtaposed against the soft sheen of a Beach Boys vocal. Although it pervades much of their early work, it wasn't until the group's later recordings that the integration of the technique for rhythmic ornamentation reached its apex. "There is a tremendous amount of doo-wop and R & B influence sprinkled throughout *Pet Sounds*," Johnston explains. One example occurs during "I'm Waiting for the Day," when Love enriches the group's high-pitched harmony line ("Aah, aah, aah") with a bass-heavy "Duh-duh, do-duh-duh."

Originally, "God Only Knows" was mixed with a vocal tag on which family and friends (Terry Melcher, Brian's wife Marilyn Wilson, and her sister Diane Rovell) intone a repetitive "bop-bop-bop-bop" line under the lush harmony round sung by Carl, Brian, and Bruce. Although it was removed from the final mix, the interpolation was a direct nod to the pulsating rhythm of street-corner harmony. (This "a cappella ending" version of the song appears on *The Pet Sounds Sessions* boxed set.)

The most striking bit of doo-wop on *Pet Sounds* comes during "I Know There's an Answer." Here, a series of lazily phrased "Aaah, di-di-di-di-di-da's" shadow Al Jardine's lead throughout the song. Then, just after the third chorus, Mike performs a lugubrious vocal "break" ("Ba doo-be-doo-be-dooooo")—a brief but memorable tag that leads into the instrumental finale.

In addition to the Coasters, the Beach Boys listened to and borrowed from several other contemporary vocal groups, the Everly Brothers in particular. "Some of our favorite Everly Brothers songs were, like, *all* of the Everly Brothers songs," says Mike Love. "The ones I can remember us doing a lot were 'Dream,' 'Bird Dog,' and 'Devoted to You.' They sang beautiful harmony, and that really attracted us." (As a tribute, the Beach Boys included a cozy harmony- and guitar- version of the duo's Top 10 hit "Devoted to You" on their 1965 album *Beach Boys' Party!*)

Brian's admiration for studio wizard Phil Spector is well documented, and while Spector's primary effect on Brian was technical, two of the producer's celebrated girl groups caught Brian's ear: the Crystals and the Ronettes.

The Crystals were the impetus for Spector's "Wall of Sound," and songs such as "Da Doo Ron Ron," "There's No Other (Like My Baby)," and "Then He Kissed Me" brought new textures to pop music. But it was the Ronettes who performed the song that Brian calls his all-time favorite: "Be My Baby." "When I first heard 'Be My Baby' in my car, I had to pull over to the side of the street. It blew my mind," he said. What surely captivated Brian was the sound of Ronnie Bennett's vocal lead floating atop the two-part harmony of her sister (Estelle Bennett) and cousin (Nedra Talley). The record—a pulsating ode to the power of young lust— embodies the best of Spector's fastidious, unorthodox production values.

Although he never made a point of publicly singling them out, Brian also admired Frankie Valli and the Four Seasons. "When 'Sherry' came out, Brian made us learn it in the bathroom 15 minutes before a show, and made us do it live because he loved the Four Seasons," remembered David Marks. Although Valli's falsetto was more strident and nasal than Wilson's, the Four Seasons offered another sound texture from which Brian could draw. Illustrating this are the saxophone voicings on the *Pet Sounds* song "Here Today," which are comparable to the characteristic, honking sax lines on the Four Seasons' "Opus 17 (Don't You Worry 'Bout Me")." On an alternate mix of "God Only Knows," made two days after the original session, Brian overdubbed a Four Seasons-style saxophone solo on the bridge, although he later dropped it in favor of the breathtaking vocal break heard on the released version.

The Freshmen Connection

While rock 'n' roll had a major effect on the band, it was the Four Freshmen—a silky smooth jazz ensemble identified more with the straitlaced sensibilities of his parents' generation than the rock 'n' roll-based preferences of Brian's own—who had the greatest role in shaping the Beach Boys' sound. Brian recalled the day he first heard their 1958 album *Voices in Love* in a local record store. "I listened to the whole album in the [listening] booth. I walked out, and I said, 'Please can I have it, Mommy?' I was so out of my mind after hearing that Four Freshmen thing. I'd come home from school and go, 'Aw, fuck doing homework. I'm gonna go listen to the Four Freshmen!'"

Freshmen manager Bill Wagner (a Capitol Records producer) remembers Brian showing up at the group's Los Angeles office, proudly demonstrating his knowledge of their music. "Brian was about 16 when he first appeared at our office. My secretary said, 'There's a young man named Brian Wilson here, and he wants to talk to you.' Brian came in and we sat and talked. 'Could I just sit here and absorb?' he asked.

I said, 'Sure. There's nothing that happens here that is a secret. The only thing that may prompt me to move you is a fire in the building!' Ten or fifteen minutes went by, and Brian said to me, 'You know, I know every note of every Freshmen record that you've got out—all four parts.' I said, 'Gee, Brian, that's wonderful!' 'Yeah,' he said. 'Test me.' I wasn't going to test him. 'No, Brian—I trust you. If you say you know it, you know it.' Well, he was insistent. 'No. I need to prove it,' he said. 'I can't prove it to anybody that I know, so I want to prove it to you, and maybe you can tell the Freshmen about it.' How could I argue with that? I pulled out a song called 'The Day Isn't Long Enough,' which was one of the toughest arrangements the guys ever did—it was a head arrangement, as many of their early things were, since none of them wrote music. I put the record on, looked at Brian, and said, 'OK, prove yourself.' We played it four times, and Brian sang it four times—once for each part. And not only did he sing all the parts correctly, he sang them all in tune. I said, 'Good Lord, Brian—you're something else! You ought to have a group.' His answer was sure and direct. 'That's why I'm here—you're gonna show me how to do it.'"

Like the Beach Boys, the Four Freshmen was a family group comprised of four members. The quartet was well schooled; their harmonizing was based on solid music theory—and eight good ears. "We realized that there was more to singing harmony than just what the piano played," says founding member Ross Barbour. "You can't get beautiful overtones if you sing the notes a piano plays; you've got to tweak the vocal notes, making them a bit sharp or flat in certain places. Then, you must go for those chords with a distinctive coloration in them, like major sevenths and flatted ninths. Some of those 'far out' chords can make such pretty sounds when you sing them. It can make your hair stand up when a chord rings. We sang those chords because they harmonized and made overtones in our ears."

The ringing chords and splendid overtones were the keys to the Four Freshmen's pleasing vocal harmony. "The ringing of the chords is what Brian Wilson fell in love with—he was charmed by this sound," Barbour explains. "On 'Now You Know,' we created a chordal tension where the notes and chords are pulled together tightly like a chain, in which the harmonies ring on each other."

Although the best performers make it seem simple, there's a good measure of technical logic behind fine vocal harmony. "Good vocals are much more in tune than the keyboard," explains barbershop vocal arranger David Wright. "The keyboard is out of tune by virtue of Bach's tempered scale; it allows for modulation, but it doesn't really present any given key in tune. A good vocal ensemble finds that finer tuning. Even though they may have instruments in the background, the three or four voices that are finding each other find those correct mathematical relationships. Therefore, you get a kind of stability that we call 'ring and lock.' When the Beach Boys hit a good major chord it locked, and sounded just beautiful."

The "ringing" of a chord is also known as expanded sound. "In the vocal world, when we talk about expanded sound, it means that even though there are four voices, it sounds like more than four voices," Wright explains. "This happens because the voices are tuned well, and they're matched in terms of their timbre and the word sounds. It gives the impression of more voices than are actually there, because they're supporting each other's harmonics. The reinforced overtones give the harmony a bigger sound than what you'd expect out of so few voices."

Heredity is another important factor. "There haven't been many great vocal groups that didn't have some family in them," Barbour asserts. "The vocal sound is similar by heredity and the pronunciation is the same, because the members grew up in the same environment. Pronunciation is key; if you're not all pronouncing the words the same, it sounds wrong when you sing it. Also, when you're young, you learn how to get along with your brother or your sister, and when you build a vocal group, your biggest challenge is to stay together and get along. It appears that the Wilson brothers learned how to solve family problems through singing."

The Murry Factor

The velvety harmonies the Beach Boys created became an instant sensation, and success came quickly as the group recorded one chart-topping hit after another. Among the favorites cut between 1962 and 1964 were "Surfin' Safari," "409," "Surfin' USA," "Surfer Girl," "Catch a Wave," "Little Deuce Coupe," "In My Room," "Fun, Fun, Fun," "Don't Worry Baby," "The Warmth of the Sun," "Be True to Your School," "I Get Around," "All Summer Long," and "Wendy." Along with the songs of Lennon and McCartney, they are among the most recognizable tunes in all of pop music.

Much of the band's early success can be attributed to Murry Wilson's tenacious drive. As their manager and chief business advisor, he plugged the band relentlessly, and set up a lucrative publishing company (Sea of Tunes) to handle Brian's growing catalog of songs. But while he could enchant disc jockeys and record promoters with disarming ease, his abrasive personality didn't endear him to their associates. "A lot of people didn't like Murry, and I didn't particularly like him as a person," said Chuck Britz. "But I liked him for what he believed in doing for the guys. He cared about the guys— he really did, in his own way. Murry was a hard-nosed devil, but he cared about them."

In the studio, Murry freely asserted his opinion—even though Brian took the lead as producer. But Chuck Britz found a way to keep him at bay. "I got along with Murry, because I made him *think* I was doing what he wanted to do," he said. "I set up a talk-back button, and I gave him two pots on the end of the board, and said, 'Now here are the vocals— you do what you want.' [But the pots] were deader than hell, because I didn't want to fight with him. He'd say, 'Surge!' [meaning that Britz should increase the level of the vocals], and I'd say, 'There they are—surge!' and turn the monitor up. And he'd say, 'God—this is great! Guys, you're doing great! You're doing great!' But he wasn't really doing anything."

Concert promoter Fred Vail summarized the essence of Murry Wilson for journalist Timothy White. "The guy's like an old-fashioned drill sergeant," he explained. "He's loving and protective, and at the same time gruff and very, very assertive. He can be humble and he can be arrogant. He can be a proud father and he can be a screaming manager. He's very physical—walking the tightrope between father and uncle, manager and taskmaster is too difficult for him." Murry—with Vail's assistance—kept the Beach Boys on a rigorous and profitable touring schedule, which helped boost record sales. Their efforts worked: the Beach Boys' records virtually flew off the shelves.

Of the eight albums recorded between October 1962 and December 1964, six made the *Billboard* Top 10: *Surfin' USA* (released in March 1963) reached number 2, *Little Deuce Coupe* (released in October 1963) hit number 4, *Surfer Girl* (released in September 1963) made it to number 7, and *All Summer Long* (released in July 1964) climbed to number 4. *The Beach Boys' Christmas Album* (released in November 1964) topped out at number 6 on *Billboard's* Christmas chart. Ironically, their weakest album of the period, *Beach Boys Concert* (recorded live in Sacramento and released in 1964) shot to number 1 and remained on *Billboard's* Top 200 album chart for over a year. *Shut Down, Vol.* 2 (released in March 1964) peaked at a respectable number 13, while their first album, *Surfin' Safari* (released in October 1962) stopped short at number 32.

These albums produced seven Top 20 singles: "Surfin' Safari" (number 14), "Surfin' USA" (number 3), "Surfer Girl" (number 7), "Little Deuce Coupe" (number 15), "Fun, Fun, Fun" (number 5), "I Get Around" (number 1), and "Be True to Your School" (number 6). A Christmas single, "The Man with All the Toys," backed with "Blue Christmas," hit number 3 on the seasonal charts. In addition, two singles recorded and issued in 1964 (and later released on the 1965 album *The Beach Boys Today!*) also charted well: "When I Grow Up (To Be a Man)" reached number 9, and "Dance, Dance, Dance" topped out at number 8.

While the last month of the year would signal serious changes in the band, by 1964, the Beach Boys were firmly entrenched as one of the most successful American pop groups. The band had come a long way from Brian Wilson and Al Jardine's original dream. "When the Beach Boys started, I wanted us to be a folk group," Jardine said. "As it turns out, the group *has* become America's balladeers regarding music; the folk myths, the experience of this country."

turning points

"Everything that is truly great and inspiring is created by the individual who can labor in freedom."
Albert Einstein

"Wilson is growing."
Brian Wilson, 1966

The beginning of 1964 found the Beach Boys at their commercial peak, having garnered an impressive string of hit singles and albums. They were in demand, performing scores of concerts to meet the unquenchable thirst of a growing fan base. And in between personal appearances, Brian and Mike Love were writing new songs, striving to keep the band in the studio and the record label—which was constantly demanding new product—off their backs. The frenetic pace took its toll on Brian, who was on the verge of physical collapse. By December, his breakdown was complete.

The Breakdown
In 1983, Carl Wilson discussed Brian's emotional meltdown with journalist Geoffrey Himes. "This guy [allegedly Loren Schwartz] had turned Brian on to LSD, and he just wasn't set up for it—he couldn't handle it. The pressure of writing, producing, and performing all had a cumulative effect on him. Earlier that year, the group had decided they didn't want to work with my dad anymore. There were some fatherhood issues he wasn't willing to let go of. It's hard to have someone

bossing you around and working for you too. All of these pressures and the chemicals took Brian apart."

Brian's drug use was surely exacerbated by his tumultuous relationship with Murry Wilson, whose harsh, narcissistic personality bred contempt and disdain in his children. While Murry was among the Beach Boys' staunchest supporters, his obsessive quest for control inhibited their growth. By mid-1964, his dictatorial demeanor had become a serious impediment. When he was in the booth there was tension in the air, and his visits to the studio became infrequent.

Although Brian outwardly accepted his father's constant meddling, petty squabbles erupted with greater frequency, forcing him to admit a professional divorce was imminent and unavoidable. As difficult as it was, Brian realized that none of his ideas could be fully realized with a man like Murry in the picture.

Why was Murry so difficult? Often it was ego and pride that dictated his response to the people and situations around him. At home, he was having marital trouble (he and Audree had separated in late 1964), and there was some evidence that he was drinking excessively. He may also have been disillusioned by the growth of the Beach Boys, and of Brian in particular. His son was moving in new directions and reaching outside the group for support—and Murry perceived that as a threat. Two fractious incidents led to his dismissal as the Beach Boys' manager.

The first occurred on April 2, 1964, at the recording session for "I Get Around," during which an obstreperous Murry badgered Brian and Dennis. The heckling ended in a brawl. "Murry and Dennis got into a big argument," explained Chuck Britz. "Dennis just hauled off and swung at Murry, putting his fist right through the wall. That's the only time they ever had a physical fight, as far as I know—after that happened, things kind of calmed down." But Brian was shocked and hurt. "You've gone too damned far," he shouted, pushing his father back. "You're fired!"

It wasn't until months later, after the band's legal transfer of their business affairs to an outside agent, that Murry was welcomed back to the studio—as a visitor. On February 24, 1965, he showed up mildly intoxicated and proceeded to interfere with the group's rerecording of "Help Me, Rhonda." "Let's sing from our hearts. Come on, fellas. We need the honest projection that we used to have," he chided, slipping back into his former role as their producer. As Audree and the band watched, Murry's words turned sour, his tone accusatory. "When you guys make too much money, you start thinking you're going to make everything a hit."

The terse exchange, captured on tape by Chuck Britz, continued:

Murry: *Now listen, let me tell you something. When you guys get so big that you can't sing from your heart, you're going downhill.*

Brian: *Downhill.*

Murry: *Downhill! Son, son. I'm sorry. I've protected you for 22 years, but I can't go on if you're not going to listen to an intelligent man, against many people trying to hurt you.*

Brian: *Are you going now?*

Murry: *I . . . no . . . this is awfully unfair for you to . . .*

Brian: *Are you going or staying? I just wanna know.*

Murry: *What do you want? If you want to fight for success, I'll go all out.*

Brian: *No, we don't want to do that.*

Murry: *You think you got it made?*

Brian: *No, we don't. We would like to record in an atmosphere of calmness and you're not presenting that.*

Moments later, Murry fled the studio. The outburst marked the end of his tenure as the band's manager, advisor, and nominal producer. His sole business connection to the Beach Boys would remain Sea of Tunes, the publishing company he'd formed for them in March 1962.

For Brian, who internalized everything while quietly tolerating his father's abhorrent behavior, it wasn't a pleasant situation. Although their relationship was stormy, Brian maintained respect for his father, seeing past the surly attitude that Murry inflicted on his children. Indeed, he has often spoken of Murry with admiration.

"He had a lot of balls," Brian said. "With him, everything was 'punch.' He really tackled things—really got behind them." But inside, Brian craved his father's approval. To compensate for Murry's lack of affection, he salved his wounds with music—and with drugs.

Flirting with Danger

Already experimenting with marijuana, Brian began using LSD at least a year before starting work on *Pet Sounds*. "I had one retreat before *Pet Sounds*, which was LSD, and then about a year's worth of paranoia," he once admitted. Tragically, his continued abuse of the drug during the making of *Pet Sounds* contributed to the mental ills that irrevocably damaged his psyche.

At first, indications that Brian was struggling emotionally were small. While departing for an Australian tour in November 1964, he experienced an anxiety attack. When he arrived at his destination, he calmed himself by proposing to his girlfriend, Marilyn Rovell. The pair got married on December 7, 1964.

Marilyn was devoted and supportive, but she soon noticed a change in her husband. Once attentive and outgoing, he became detached, and seemed to disregard her emotional needs. Often he would disappear from their Hollywood apartment for days without explanation. Marilyn also discovered that Brian was using marijuana, which drove them further apart.

On a late-December flight en route to a concert in Houston, Brian finally lost his composure. Within minutes of departing Los Angeles, his fragile nerves succumbed. He began rocking in his seat, then fell to the floor. "I can't take it!" he shouted at Al Jardine and Carl Wilson. "I just can't take it! Don't you understand? I'm not getting off this plane!" They persuaded him to disembark, but after performing that night, he secluded himself in the hotel. He flew back to California the next day, where Audree met him at the airport. Their visit to his vacant boyhood home in Hawthorne provided a temporary catharsis; it was the last time he ever went back.

According to Mike Love, there was no sign of depression or mental illness in Brian's past to forecast the erratic behavior that surfaced in 1964. "I saw none of that when Brian was younger—none," he says. "I think it had to do with the drugs. Had Brian not done psychedelic drugs, he may never have developed the type of illness that he did. My major regret— not only for Brian, but for the rest of the group and the fans—is that there would have been a lot more brilliant music had Brian not suffered from his indulgences."

Love's assertion is not far off the mark. As clinical psychologist Dr. Michael Gerson explains, there is a clear connection between substance abuse and emotional instability. "Brian was not alone in experiencing the way that hallucinogenic drugs can unleash underlying emotional pathology waiting to burst forth," he says. "In the 1960s, many people were unpleasantly surprised by the often paranoid—and at times delusional—effects caused by hallucinogens such as marijuana, hashish, and, more frequently, LSD. But it's important to know that such drugs do not 'create' the kind of emotional difficulties that Brian Wilson experienced; they provoke its onset. In his case, it can be assumed that were it not for the drugs, the significant stress Brian perceived himself to be under would have, sooner or later, resulted in the emotional distress that his drug-taking set into motion."

How did the band cope with Brian's strange behavior? "Unbeknownst to us, Brian had a mental illness called paranoid schizophrenia," Love explains. "We didn't know about this disease; none of us were psychiatrists or psychologists.

We were young guys who were singing songs and having a great time achieving astounding success. When Brian started to show signs of mental instability, we didn't know what it was. We thought maybe he was homesick, or that he wasn't cut out for the road."

Moment of Truth

Although it rocked the group to its core, Brian's nervous breakdown afforded him the chance to grow creatively, and it signaled the start of his physical break from the Beach Boys. "One night, I told the guys I wasn't going to perform on stage anymore," Brian said at the time. "I told them that I foresaw a beautiful future for the Beach Boys [as a] group, but the only way we could achieve it was if they did their job, and I did mine. That night, when I gave them the news of my decision, they all broke down. I'd already gone through my breakdown, and now it was their turn.

"I was run down mentally and emotionally because I was running around, jumping on jets, [doing] one-night stands, singing, planning, teaching. [It was] to the point where I had no peace of mind, no chance to actually sit down and think or even rest. I was so mixed up and overworked. I knew I should have stopped going on tours much earlier to do justice to our recordings."

Brian's brother Carl proved to be far more than a competent guitarist or a fine vocalist. Ultimately, he became Brian's confidante—a true "brother confessor." After Brian left the Beach Boys, he was the glue that held the group together.

From the start, they shared an undeniable bond, and Brian always relied heavily on Carl's musical opinion. "When I was eight years old, he was teaching me arrangements," Carl explained to Brian's friend, writer David Leaf, in 1996. "It was literally, 'Mom, make Carl sing.' I learned how to do very complex harmonies and voicings when I was very young, and I learned how to do them quickly so I could go out and play." As time passed and the group gained success, Brian increasingly turned to him for advice. "I've always been the one who worked real closely with Brian," he said in 1983. "I was his sounding board; I was his underling. I always tagged along. In addition to being one of the players in the studio, I worked with him in the control room, because he wanted my ear."

Because of their closeness, Carl became Brian's rock during this uncertain time. "Good old Carl was the only guy who never got into a bad emotional scene," Brian explained in 1966. "He just sat there and didn't get uptight about it. He always kept a cool head. If it weren't for Carl, it's hard to say where we'd be. He's the greatest stabilizing influence in the group."

By this point, Brian had begun using studio musicians for recordings, and the touring band was financing the recording band. Concerts provided visibility and guaranteed record sales, and disbanding the group was not an option. "We had the choice of continuing or not continuing," Carl explained. "We just felt, 'This is too much fun to stop.' It got the group to discipline itself and to really do good work on the road. I assumed leadership; it seemed natural. It got to the point where I knew it would get done if I did it."

To fill Brian's void the band hired studio guitarist Glen Campbell, who'd played on a number of their records. But Campbell soon discovered that he preferred the comfort of the recording studio to the rigors of the road. After a short stint of one-nighters, he declined the band's offer to make him a full-fledged Beach Boy. When Capitol Records offered him the chance to record as a solo recording artist, he jumped at the opportunity.

Repaying Campbell for his contribution to the band, Brian wrote and produced one of the musician's earliest singles, "Guess I'm Dumb." While the recording augured the elaborate productions that Brian would soon create, the song didn't jell with Campbell's country music audience. New material was found, and soon Campbell was storming the charts with hits including "Wichita Lineman," "Galveston," and "By the Time I Get to Phoenix"—songs that made him a household name.

The Beach Boys' replacement for Campbell was Bruce Johnston, a young artist carving his own niche on the exploding studio scene. In addition to contributing to numerous sessions and recording solo albums under his own name, Johnston was a part of two groundbreaking groups with Terry Melcher: a surf duo named Bruce & Terry, and the Rip-Chords whose "Hey Little Cobra" was one of Columbia Records' first rock 'n' roll hits. In addition to writing and performing, Johnston was also a budding Columbia Records staff producer.

In April 1965 Johnston began joining the Beach Boys in the recording studio; "California Girls" marks his vocal debut on a Beach Boys record. "The 'California Girls' session was like a first date," Johnston recalls. "I was thrilled! Brian realized that he could have a new vocal texture—another Beach Boys instrument—if he added me in. And so, I found myself in front of the microphone, another color for Brian's palette."

Freed from the pressure of traveling, Brian regrouped, spending his time writing while the Beach Boys toured. The situation forced him to work in seclusion, and, although the year preceding *Pet Sounds* was creatively stimulating, it was saturated with emotional peril. Brian's eventual downturn was a direct result of his drug use. "Brian was so sensitive," his brother Carl explained to journalist Colin McEnroe in 1981. "He was just the wrong person to go popping LSD."

Acid Trip

While LSD (lysergic acid diethylamide) became the fashionable drug of the 1960s, it was nearly 25 years old by the time of the decade's debilitating drug revolution. Although its effects had been known since 1943, social use of the drug didn't begin until the 1950s, when Dr. Oscar Janiger, a Los Angeles-based psychiatrist, began administering the drug as an experimental tool to study the mind's creative potential. Janiger provided the chemical to numerous artists, musicians, actors, and writers. Among the most celebrated writers to dabble with the drug were Aldous Huxley (who described the experience as " . . . without question the most extraordinary and significant experience this side of the Beatific Vision") and Jack Kerouac (who said his trip " . . . was a definite satori—full of psychic clairvoyance").

Like surfing, LSD had a strong allure, and it quickly seeped into the era's music. In 1960 the Gamblers (a California surf band that included Bruce Johnston on piano) recorded "LSD 25," and the drug appeared on both the east and west coast underground markets. By early 1965, the first major wave of street acid became available. In 1967 the

Beatles recorded "Lucy in the Sky with Diamonds," a song many considered to be a thinly veiled homage to the psychedelic subculture proliferating across the country (a point the Beatles denied).

Questions regarding the substance's deleterious effects were raised. LSD causes a flood of concurrent emotions, often including extreme terror, as well as delusions, hallucinations, and an altered perception of time and space. A sensory "crossover" effect—in which people *hear* colors and *see* sounds—is common. Adverse reactions are not unusual; a bad "trip" can precipitate a frightening sense of losing control, a fear of dying or going insane, and deep despair.

The drug was outlawed in 1968—three years after Brian embarked on his first acid trip. "I did my dose of LSD," Brian said in 1976. "It shattered my mind, and I came back, thank God, in I don't know how many pieces."

It is not certain who introduced Brian to LSD, but many close to him believe it was Loren Schwartz, a familiar figure on the fringes of the Los Angeles music scene. Lyricist Tony Asher remembers Brian attending social gatherings at Schwartz's home. "Loren Schwartz had been a classmate of mine at Santa Monica City College, and we'd remained friends. He would have parties at his house—he knew people in the music business, from going to clubs. Loren was outgoing and fairly charismatic, and after a show was over, he'd go up to the stage before the guys left, and talk to them. He would invite these people over to his place. He was also a connection for marijuana—and beyond."

"I only smoked dope at his house. Everybody was doing that sort of thing in the open—it was perfectly acceptable.

But then there were people sneaking off to other little rooms doing what I'm told was probably LSD, because there wasn't a lot of other stuff being used at the time. But that was being done in private. Occasionally, I would see Brian there—but he never stayed for very long. It was strange. You almost wondered why he came at all, because he'd come alone and sit in the corner. People would talk to him, and then move away and talk to somebody else, and he'd just sit there alone. After a while he'd get up and leave."

Brian was frequently partying with Schwartz, and began using drugs regularly. In 1966 Brian discussed his progressive use with writer and journalist Tom Nolan. "About a year ago, I had what I consider a very religious experience. I took LSD—a full dose of LSD—and later, another time, I took a smaller dose. And I learned a lot of things, like patience, understanding. I can't teach you or tell you what I learned from taking it, but I consider it a very religious experience."

Later that same year, Brian divulged the extent of his use. "I've been through a zillion bags, more bags in the last year than you can believe," he said. "Each little adventure taught me something about myself and people and life. I've been through so many changes. And I went on pills because I was curious, not so much for kicks as for exploration. Some pills won't hurt you, but stimulate your mind. Including the psychedelics."

Bill Wagner remembers a day when Brian visited his Capitol Records office to pose a serious question about the drug. "It was the middle of 1965, and Brian came in and closed the door. He said, 'What do you think of LSD?' I said, 'How long have you been on it?' 'How do you know I'm on it?' he asked. 'Well, Brian. You're one of the most intelligent people I know, and you wouldn't ask a dumb question like that unless you want me to tell you it's all right—and it isn't.' 'But I hear all these incredible sounds,' he said. I tried to reason with him. 'Brian, let me tell you something. I have a friend whose son is a psychiatric resident in the Department of Psychology at UCLA. He was over at our house, and he gave me a long lecture about the effects of LSD. The doctors are seeing an increasing number of young people who are dosed out on it. Let me put you together with Duke [Fisher], so he can fill you in on what this stuff does to you.' I got them together for lunch, and afterward Duke told me, 'I don't know if he is savable. He gives me the impression he's been on it for a while, and he's entirely enamored of it.' About a week later, Brian came back to my office and asked me to come down to Studio B. When we got down there, he said to me, 'Let me play something that I hear when I've been on LSD.' He sat down at the piano and played one note. He described what he was hearing. That's when I knew he was in trouble."

At home, Marilyn Wilson tried in vain to persuade her husband that drugs—and the "friends" who supplied them to him—were destroying his brilliance. It would be the first of many such interventions that those close to Brian would attempt during the next 20 years, and although she had acted out of love for him, many of his friends treated Marilyn like a pariah because of it. "People are nice to me now," she says. "But in those days, they would act like I wasn't there, like I was in the way. Guess what—I was! I was the one who was there watching all of them. I was always watching and assessing what was really going on there. What were they doing that they didn't want me to see? They were introducing artificial stimulants to Brian.

"Those drugs did some incredible damage—damage from which there was no return. I tried day and night for years to shield Brian from this destruction, but he was just as creative this way as he was musically. I tried to find doctors who could deal with him, at a time when he was in such demand. It was a time when Brian was young, energetic, and working nonstop. My search for doctors lasted years and years. Brian's ability to 'put on' these professionals made it difficult to find someone who could deal with him on his own level. I am tired of hearing that Brian's problems were never addressed, for those who say that were not there, and do not know the truth!"

Glen Campbell (a recovered substance abuser) witnessed Brian's plunge into hell. "I hated to see what Brian did to his life," Campbell told writer Gary Terratzo. "It was tragic. You just keep doing that stuff long enough and it will definitely destroy your body and your system. I'd talk to Brian, but it seemed like after he'd come back from the drug scene he'd lost a couple of steps."

Assessing the situation almost forty years later, it is painfully clear that drugs took a merciless toll on Brian Wilson: emotionally, physically, and mentally. Many believe that drugs are responsible for the difficulties he encountered during subsequent decades, and a mountain of scientific data supports that theory. Because his drug use was still in its earliest stages during the *Pet Sounds* period, Brian hadn't yet descended into the abyss that would rob his life of nearly 25 prime years. At the time, he felt it enhanced what he was writing for *Pet Sounds*, saying, "The LSD brought out some of the insecurities in me, which I think went into the music. It was so sensitive."

Summer of '65

Although *Pet Sounds* was for the most part recorded in 1966, the seeds that gave it bloom were sown and fertilized during the previous 12 months. It was a period of intense growth that signaled a remarkable creative metamorphosis. During that rocky year, Chuck Britz saw Brian rally as he turned to music for relief. "When Brian finally got off the road, I'd get calls in the middle of the night, and a lot of times I'd go pick him up and we'd go to the studio. I'd call in four or five musicians—at 12:30 or 1:00 in the morning. Nothing ever happened, but for Brian it was a confidence builder."

Following his cataclysmic breakdown, Brian began intensive "music therapy," spending most of his time devising ideas and melodies for the mature projects he planned to do—with and without the Beach Boys. "I wanted to write [songs] containing more than one level," he explained at the time. "Eventually, I would like to see longer singles—so that the song can be more meaningful. A song can, for instance, have movements—in the same way as a classical concerto—only capsulized."

His philosophy mirrored a trend born of the growing folk movement. "The change comes at a time in music history when what I call 'pippity-pop' was happening," explains veteran producer Phil Ramone. "There was nothing negative about it—it was just pop music, and there wasn't much substance to it. No one had dug into heavy lyrics until the mid-'60s—the Bob Dylans, the Peter, Paul and Marys—and those in the folk community were the only ones creating 'message' songs with political statements. Songs like 'If I Had a Hammer,' and that kind of stuff. With standard pop music, it was two minutes and ten seconds, and out you go. Radio was far more formula-driven then than it is now."

Although Brian's transition from writing car and surf songs to writing studious ones had begun much earlier (we can hear it in tunes such as "In My Room" and "The Warmth of the Sun"—both from 1963), it exploded in 1965 and culminated one year later with *Pet Sounds*. "Surfing and surf music were very much a reflection of that particular period in our lives," Carl Wilson said in 1966. "We are trying to be just as honest in our present compositions. They are a reflection—in musical terms—of our thoughts and ideas now. We believe in God as a kind of universal consciousness. God is love, God is you, God is me, God is everything right here in this room. It's a spiritual concept, which inspires a great deal of our music."

Marilyn Wilson recalls the point at which she perceived a change in Brian's music. "I saw a progression from the surf music when Brian noticed that people in other studios were expanding their studio sounds. Of course, he was so impressed with Phil Spector and the 'Wall of Sound' he was creating. It inspired Brian—his musical mind just took off on its own path. The difference was that Brian heard the music, the different instruments, the harmonies of the voices, and the production at the same time. He wrote, arranged, and produced it all! It was all there in his mind, and people would just look at him in amazement. They would want to be around Brian, just to get a glimpse of the man. Maybe they thought it would rub off on them. He soon had the freedom to make his music as he pleased, with no limitations—except for the people who thought he should just continue to write in the surf style. Sometimes it was hard for him to incorporate it all into one, but he did it. Many of his songs were simple, yet complicated. It was always interesting to see what he would come up with next."

A portent of the direction Brian was heading in surfaced in mid-1965 with the arrival of two albums: *The Beach Boys Today!* and *Summer Days (and Summer Nights!!)*. The songs (especially those on *The Beach Boys Today!*) exhibit a unified lyrical theme: the wonder of adolescent love and the expression of tender, pleading affection. They also reveal new depths in performance, production, and—most of all—arrangement and instrumentation. "Starting with these albums and following straight through to *Pet Sounds*, you hear adjacent things—like a woodwind quartet with an accordion underneath," explains Phil Ramone. "We hadn't heard that before—not in pop music. Claude Thornhill or Gil Evans might have used these voicings in their jazz arrangements, but from this point on Brian began introducing some incredible instrumental clusters to mainstream pop music."

Brian himself recognized the transition. "By May, the LP [*The Beach Boys Today!*] was number 4 on the album charts, while at the same time [the song] 'Help Me, Rhonda' was number 1," he said. "It seemed business as usual. Except that there were some subtle but noticeable changes in the music. The whole second side of *The Beach Boys Today!* had been written and arranged while I was high. Compared to previous Beach Boys albums, the music was slower, more plaintive, and emotional. The chord patterns were more complex, the production denser, richer in sound, and my thinking with regard to making records was different. Able to break down songs to precise little increments, I began to deal with each instrument individually, stacking sounds one at a time."

The Beach Boys Today!, which was released in March, featured an array of fun, danceable rock 'n' roll tunes, including "Do You Wanna Dance?," "Good to My Baby," "Help Me, Rhonda," and "Dance, Dance, Dance." But the real treasures are the absorbing string of refined Brian Wilson–Mike Love tunes nestled among them: "Please Let Me Wonder," "Kiss Me Baby," "She Knows Me Too Well," and "When I Grow Up (To Be a Man)"—all of which rival the best of songs on *Pet Sounds*. Lyrically, the tunes on both albums, and on *The Beach Boys Today!* in particular, have far more substance than the sophomoric ones in which the Beach Boys declare their love for a girl, a car, or the surf. While his contemporaries wrote idealistically about social issues, Brian turned inward for inspiration. His emotions—and the words that described them—were dramatic, intense, and personal.

What was the impetus for change? What inspired Brian and his collaborators to dig deep inside and use their innermost feelings to articulate the elusive powers of love?

Until the mid-1960s, mainstream pop music was written and produced according to broad commercial standards. While a handful of songwriters (such as Burt Bacharach and Hal David) had begun breaking free to create inventive styles that fulfilled both the commercial expectations of the industry and their own creative needs, most—including the Beatles and the Beach Boys—stuck with the prescribed formula. It wasn't until Bob Dylan and other pioneers of the folk-rock movement came along that writers felt liberated enough to bare their souls—personally and politically—for the sake of their art.

Both pop culture and the political maelstrom swirling around him had a serious effect on the growth and shape of Brian's music in the mid-1960s. "In November 1963 John F. Kennedy was killed. Culture changed, and kids began to take control," explains Hal Lifson. "The young kids of the late '50s were teenagers in the mid-'60s, and they were looking for music that was more sophisticated than the soda-fountain pop-rock they were hearing in the early 1960s. As these changes occurred, Brian embarked on an insular, spiritual quest to define himself through his music, using it to communicate his deepest thoughts and concerns. He reached for a higher level, and achieved it."

Although it didn't boil over until 1965, poetic emotion had been locked up inside of Brian for a long time. "People always thought Brian was a good-time guy until he started releasing those heavy, searching songs on *Pet Sounds*," Dennis Wilson said. "But that stuff was closer to his own personality and perceptions. By the time people get close to an accurate picture of Brian Wilson—if ever—he's gonna be far beyond them again."

For Brian, the change was personal: it was a form of existentialism that allowed him to project himself through the music. On *The Beach Boys Today!*, Brian writes and sings in the first person, allowing the songs to mirror the emotions he experiences—the very same ones that he knows all young men find hard to express.

"Please Let Me Wonder" sympathetically conveys the vulnerable pathos that is the bane of every boy's existence, giving voice to their most coveted hopes and dreams: "Please let me wonder/If I've been the one you love." The confusing emotions of young love are laid bare as never before, couched within the safe, comforting environs of a two-and-a-half minute pop ballad.

"Kiss Me Baby" also ups the thematic ante, chronicling a repentant boyfriend's request for his lover's forgiveness. The real treat here is the tune's buttery-smooth vocal arrangement, which sports a letter-perfect interweaving of multiple parts (and which foreshadows the thick layering achieved on "God Only Knows"). Here Brian skillfully blends three distinctly different parts: the primary line ("Kiss me baby/Love to hold you . . . "), a syncopated counter line ("Kiss a little bit/Fight a little bit/Kiss a little bit/Fight a little bit") and a bass line (Mike Love intoning "Whoa, baby" underneath). The vocal glows with a rich, golden transparency.

Of the lot, "When I Grow Up (To Be a Man)" best exemplifies the musical growth heard on *The Beach Boys Today!* Lyrically, the song introduces a new form in which the protagonists (Brian and Mike) pose rhetorical questions pondering what they'll be like at different points in their lives: "Now I'm young and free, but how will it be?" "Will I look for the same things in a woman that I dig in a girl?" "Will I love my wife for the rest of my life?"

Few songwriters addressed adolescent concerns with such sincerity, and none framed their ideas as inventively as Brian and Mike did on "When I Grow Up." The song achieves a fine balance, pairing the tune's reflective lyrical theme with an upbeat arrangement. But don't be fooled: the lighthearted tone doesn't dampen the sentimentality of the message—it actually amplifies it.

Instrumentally, "When I Grow Up" features an effective combination of old sounds (surf-style rhythm and guitar) and new (harpsichord and chromatic harmonica). The chart's complexity is evident from the start, where the snare, high-hat, tom-tom, bass, and harpsichord establish a syncopated rhythmic pattern that everything else hinges on. The vocal harmonies are full and round, and small details, such as simple call and response lines and the juxtaposition of Brian's falsetto singing "It's kinda sad" against Mike's "Won't last forever" at the end, make for a lively mix. Overall, the key to the song's success is the band's simple, staccato recitation of various ages (16, 17, 18), which provides the all-important commercial hook. From beginning to end the instrumental and vocal lines interlock with a satisfying precision, effortlessly supporting and strengthening each other. More than any other recording, "When I Grow Up" anticipates the fresh approach that Brian would take in arranging *Pet Sounds*.

Conversely, "In the Back of My Mind" is a disturbing statement that one would expect to find on a post-*Pet Sounds* album such as *Smile*, or the Beatles' White Album. While "When I Grow Up" integrated the familiar Beach Boys sound into a more mature tune, "In the Back of My Mind" is the antithesis of any prescribed commercial formula—a curious experiment marking an extreme deviation for the band. The song's dissonant orchestration (which features unexpected instruments including oboe, saxophone, and strings) is haunting, and is vaguely reminiscent of the Beatles'

"Norwegian Wood." The lyrics have an aching, surreal quality (a psychedelic nod to Brian's growing psychoses?), and Dennis's lead vocal sounds "warped," as though it has been filtered through a fun-house distortion mirror. The arrangement's peculiarity makes the record downright spooky—almost too far ahead of its time.

On the other hand, *Summer Days (and Summer Nights!!)*, which was released in June 1965, three months after *The Beach Boys Today!*, is a rock-solid Beach Boys album that blends the traditional with the progressive. Of the album's twelve songs, five became classics: "Girl Don't Tell Me," "Help Me, Rhonda" (the more exciting 45-rpm rerecording), "You're So Good to Me," "Let Him Run Wild," and the recording Brian once hailed as his greatest production ever, "California Girls."

Carl Wilson believed that the album was momentous. "It was around *Summer Days* that it became evident to me that Brian was evolving very rapidly on many different levels," he told David Leaf. "If one song offered a big clue that he was taking pop music to a new level, it was 'Let Him Run Wild.' I remember first hearing the track—in the verse, there are so many different parts, themes and lines."

Like "When I Grow Up (To Be a Man)," "Let Him Run Wild" is an excellent example of the highly polished production style that Brian perfected in 1965. The interweaving of parts (guitar against guitar, guitar against moving bass lines) is masterful, and it adds a solid underpinning that's hard to beat. The bass line is far more melodic than on most pop songs, hinting that Brian may have taken a cue from Motown bassist James Jamerson, whose meaty, melodic improvisations influenced a host of musicians.

Brian always used unusual chord changes to extract heart-felt emotion, and he honed his skills to perfection on *The Beach Boys Today!* and *Summer Days (and Summer Nights!!)*. Although it doesn't stray far from the four-chord structure of a traditional pop tune, "Let Him Run Wild" is rife with major sevenths—one of the wistful-sounding chords he often used to invoke a doleful, unresolved feeling. The song also exhibits an unrestrained momentum that musically personifies its lyrical theme.

The key stylistic hallmark of Brian's writing during this period—on "Let Him Run Wild" in particular—is his dexterous use of chord extensions and outside-the-scale chord progressions. "Those extensions, anything beyond the basic 1-3-5 triad, such as the 7th in a major 7th chord, add a richness to the harmony," explains musician and author Michael Miller. "And, since extended notes bump right up against the main notes in a triad, it also imparts a degree of dissonance or tension." (For less musical readers, the 7th in a major 7th chord is just a half-step away from the root of the chord. It's the sound of playing a white note on the piano and the black note next to it, simultaneously.)

"The unusual chord progressions create a sophisticated, unexpected harmonic movement; some of Brian's progressions jump way outside the underlying key, and leave the listener temporarily unsettled in terms of where the tonal center really is, which again increases the harmonic tension in the music," Miller concludes. Tertian movement (the movement of chords or keys by thirds) amplifies the forward push one senses in "Let Him Run Wild"—another subtle yet effective trick that Brian integrated to impart motion.

With *The Beach Boys Today!* and *Summer Days (and Summer Nights!!)* Brian hit a sophisticated artistic stride while maintaining the group's phenomenal commercial success. Both albums charted well: *Today!* Reached number 4, and *Summer Days* hit number 2. They also produced a respectable slew of hit singles. In addition to "When I Grow Up" and "Dance, Dance, Dance," *Today!* yielded "Do You Wanna Dance?" (number 12), while *Summer Days* offered "The Little Girl I Once Knew" (number 20), "Help Me, Rhonda" (number 1), and "California Girls" (number 3).

A quickly made album—recorded in the studio and later overdubbed with the faux sounds of an audience of "family and friends"—offered the band a welcome break from the carefully produced albums of earlier in the year. Released in November 1965, *Beach Boys Party!* featured informal covers of tunes by the Everly Brothers, the Crystals, and Bob Dylan. The album's smash single, a last-minute addition to the lineup that was suggested by Dean Torrence of the surf duo Jan & Dean, was the Regents' "Barbara Ann"—a recording that Capitol released as a single without the Beach Boys' knowledge. (Torrence, recording with Jan Berry in another studio, had ambled into the Beach Boys session and after recommending "Barbara Ann," was invited to sing high lead on the recording.)

The Beach Boys' music was changing—lyrically, instrumentally, and conceptually—for the better, and in the States, in terms of popularity and musical achievement, the band had little competition. But that, too, changed when their salt-water-and-sunshine sound was challenged by the raw, R & B-inflected tone of the Beatles.

Intrigued by the innovative approach of their British contemporaries, Brian included three Beatles tunes on the *Party!* album: "I Should Have Known Better," "Tell Me Why," and "You've Got to Hide Your Love Away." He also vowed to top their best effort: a recently released album called *Rubber Soul.* Brian shared his dream with Marilyn. "Mar," he said confidently, "I am going to make the greatest rock album ever made."

writing the album

"I wanted to create something that I thought would bring an adequate amount of spiritual love to the world."

Brian Wilson, 1996

"We weren't concerned with writing hit records. We just wanted to write some good songs."

Tony Asher

It was a cool January morning in 1966 when advertising copywriter Tony Asher hopped into his white 1965 Porsche 356C and traveled from his apartment in West L.A. to Brian Wilson's home at 1448 Laurel Way in Beverly Hills. Two questions burned in his mind as he wove his way through the city: Why had he been chosen? And what could he expect when he arrived?

Asher was buoyed by anticipation and excited by the prospect of working with Brian Wilson. But he could never have imagined how extensively this trip would affect his life, or the literature of popular music. As Asher remembers, the invitation came as a surprise. "One morning, the phone in my office rang, and a calm voice on the other end said, 'Hello, Tony? This is Brian Wilson. I need to write an album for Capitol Records, and I don't have anybody to write it with. I'm under a lot of pressure, because we're already three months behind, and I was wondering if you wanted to work on some of the songs with me.' Now, that's like someone suddenly asking, 'Would you like fifty thousand dollars?'

"At first, I thought that someone was pulling my leg. I had told people about having met Brian Wilson, so I figured that one of the guys down the hall was calling, pretending to be him. I really did, because I figured that if something like this were to happen, someone else—not Brian—would make the call. But it didn't happen that way. *He* picked up the telephone one day and called to ask me if I wanted to work on his album.

"In the days since, I've thought to myself, 'What are the possible answers to the question—*Would you like to work on the next Beach Boys album?*' Could one conceivably defer, saying 'Oh, gosh, Brian, I'd love to, but you know, I'm just really busy right now,' or, 'I dunno, let me think about it and I'll call you back?' When Brian called, I said, 'I'd love to do it—just tell me where and when.' He seemed relieved that I'd accepted. 'Great—come out next Tuesday,' he said."

Conception and Composition

Months before calling on Tony Asher, Brian had sheltered himself inside his Beverly Hills home, determined to write the album that would rival the Beatles' *Rubber Soul*. As Marilyn Wilson recalls, his aim was true. "Brian just wanted to make—in his eyes—the most wonderful rock album ever. He did not think about what music was there on the market, or what was happening [in the industry]. His album came from his heart and soul, and was what he thought was the perfect combination of voice, music, and production. Each song was a personal symphonic creation. He was driven, and found inspiration within him to accomplish this. He was consumed with thoughts of it day and night. Somehow, at the age of 18,

I knew this was a monumental time for Brian, the music industry, and the world."

Brian's creative spirit surged during the last months of 1965, and the musical energy that spilled forth signaled his arrival as a superior expressionist. What he heard and admired in the Beatles became the catalyst for *Pet Sounds*, but his motivation for writing the songs ran much deeper. "Brian's objective in creating *Pet Sounds* was to prove to the music world that he was just as talented and competent a songwriter as Lennon or McCartney," said Hal Lifson. "He wanted to do something challenging and serious, and his biggest influences were the two powerhouses in rock music at the time: Phil Spector and the Beatles."

Brian once discussed how *Rubber Soul* prompted the creation of *Pet Sounds*. "We recognized that the Beatles had cut *Rubber Soul*, and I really wasn't quite ready for its unity— it felt like it all belonged together. *Rubber Soul* was like a folk album by the Beatles that somehow went together like no album ever made before, and I was very impressed. I had to go in there [the studio] and experiment with sounds. I really felt challenged to do it—and I followed through with it."

Released in 1965, *Rubber Soul* was an assertive step forward for both the Beatles and the rock 'n' roll genre. As producer George Martin explained to historian Mark Lewisohn, "[It] was the first album to present a new, growing Beatles to the world. For the first time we began to think of albums as art of their own, as complete entities."

Rubber Soul's emotional range—and thought-provoking lyrical slant—caught Brian's attention. One tune, the charming "Norwegian Wood (This Bird Has Flown)" affected him more than any other. The arrangement demonstrates the stark use of contrasting tones and textures—elements Brian used to maximum advantage in designing the instrumental arrangements for *Pet Sounds*. "Lennon and McCartney are fantastic," Wilson told writer and publicist Derek Taylor in 1965. "They turn out so much good material. They're very melodic—they rely on melody and harmony rather than beat. They will simplify to its skeletal form an arrangement, where I would be impelled to make it more complex. Like 'Norwegian Wood,' with one voice and a sitar. I would have orchestrated it—put in background voices—done a thousand things. But the fact that the Beatles can do things with such simplicity is what makes them so good."

In discussing *Rubber Soul's* effect on Brian, it's important to remember that the album he heard in America differed from its original British counterpart. Included on Capitol's domestic version (but not on the British release) were "It's Only Love" and "I've Just Seen a Face," another song that embodied the folksy charm that he adored.

Using *Rubber Soul* as a guide, Brian retreated to pen what would become his chef-d'oeuvre. With the solitude came introspective analysis and the music marking his triumphant liberation: "Wouldn't It Be Nice," "God Only Knows," "I Just Wasn't Made for These Times," "You Still Believe in Me," "Caroline No," and seven other tunes that would form the melodic base of *Pet Sounds*.

In a series of interviews in 1966, Brian discussed the process. "Six months ago, I bought a new house up in Beverly Hills. I arranged the house so I had a big room full of music and atmosphere, and I started to plan the new direction of the group. I wanted to move ahead in sounds and melodies and moods. For months I plotted and planned. For a month or two, I sat at either a huge Spanish table looking out over the hills, just thinking, or at the piano playing 'feels.' 'Feels' are musical ideas: riffs, bridges, fragments of themes, a phrase here and there. I can write through understanding others. The surf songs are a simple example of that—I have never surfed, but I was able to feel it through Dennis.

"It all starts with religion. I believe in God—in one God, some higher being who is better than we are. But I'm not formally religious. I simply believe in the power of the spirit and in the manifestation of this in the goodness of people. I seek out the best elements in people. People are part of my music. A lot of the songs are the results of emotional experiences, sadness and pain. Or joy, exultation, and so on. Like 'California Girls'—a hymn to youth. I find it possible to spill melodies, beautiful melodies, in moments of great despair. This is one of the wonderful things about this art form—it can draw out so much emotion, and it can channel it into notes of music in cadence. Good emotional music is never embarrassing. Music is genuine and healthy, and the stimulation I get from molding it and from adding dynamics is like nothing on earth."

1448 Laurel Way

The environment in which Brian worked was conducive to the free flow of musical ideas, and the house at 1448 Laurel Way became a haven for family, friends, and Brian's music. Marilyn Wilson has fond recollections of the home she shared with Brian and how it helped spark his outpouring of musical love. "The house was at the top of Laurel Way, a winding street off Beverly Drive. Brian loved it because of the views. The house had an open feeling, with tall ceilings. It was a 1960s house with a marble floor entrance hall that had windows looking out everywhere. There was a grassy yard on the cliffside. Brian wanted to build a swimming pool, and we designed it with a slide. We had more fun with our family and friends in that pool! I loved the bedrooms, because they were in one wing of the house, all three circling a fountain in the middle. He used one of the bedrooms as an office; he liked having an office and a desk."

Marilyn explains, "It was our first home; not a huge house—probably about 3,000 square feet—but in those days, that was large for a first home. It gave him a feeling of accomplishment to have such a grand house! He could move around from room to room and not feel enclosed, and the views inspired him. Brian loved the kitchen. During this time, he would ask me to make huge prime rib dinners, and he would invite many interesting people—and our friends— over at night. He loved food and he loved to eat, and all of this went into the making of his thoughts. I went along with it because it was fun—and hectic. I would do anything for Brian."

The months that Brian spent writing the melodies for his magnum opus represent a high point for rock 'n' roll music. Thirty-six years later, Marilyn Wilson recalls watching her husband work at writing *Pet Sounds*. "You can't imagine what it was like waking up every day with him; every day provided a new experience. You didn't know what to expect. There was no such thing as a typical day. It was never, 'OK, Mar, it's ten o'clock—we're going to bed.' Sometimes during the making of *Pet Sounds* he would be up all night long, and then he'd sleep in the morning. He was always a night person. I can't tell you how many hours he would work every day, because it was all the time, unless he was in the car. When he was home, he was either at the piano, arranging, or eating.

"The atmosphere in our house during the making of *Pet Sounds* was different than other times. Most of the time, Brian was concentrating on the concept of the album. I knew it must have been hard for him; who knew what was really going on in that mind? He had people demanding the typical [Beach Boys] sounds, yet he wanted to go further—where no other pop writer had gone. He didn't have to look for it—it was there. It was all in his head and soul. He just yearned for this wonderful music to come out of him. It was a very spiritual thing.

"As I walked through the house, I would hear Brian's music. I would never interrupt—he was working. But there were always adventures. Sometimes, at three in the morning, he would wake me up. He would say, 'Mar, Mar—you gotta come hear this!' I would get up, and as I fixed him a sandwich, Brian would play what he'd just written. I loved everything he wrote. I don't know how to explain it—it was just wonderful."

If the inspiration to write a song presented itself Brian wrote one, hammering out the melody on the piano while sketching its basic chord symbols on music paper. Later he would share the tune with a suitable lyricist, and together they would mold it into a finished song. While his approach to songwriting was basic, it reflected the brooding intensity with which he viewed life, art, and music. "I approach my music-making as something pure from the spirit, to which I can add dynamics and marketable reality," he explained. "I used to have to work at writing and producing. While we were on the road, I'd sit down and say, 'I've got to write a song. Just got to.' But that's over. Now I just wait for the 'feels.' The strange thing is that they come more often, they get better, and all of a sudden complexity has become a pleasant exercise."

Why did Brian—a skilled wordsmith—look to others for lyrics? Couldn't he, better than anyone, understand the emotional objective of his songs? Although he could have easily written the lyrics himself, Brian craved the fresh perspective of a well-suited collaborator. "It was Brian who composed the music and came up with the concepts for the songs," says Marilyn Wilson. "But he loved having people write the lyrics with him, because he felt they could add sophistication to his ideas."

Enter Asher

Brian knew from the start that *Pet Sounds* would be important, and to help him grace his melodies with the appropriate words he turned to Tony Asher, a young ad man not yet known for his songwriting. Admittedly, his choice was unusual. But by 1965, the successful "surf-and-turf" sound that Brian had perfected with Mike Love, Gary Usher, and disk jockey-turned songwriter friend Roger Christian was getting stale, and he was looking to establish himself as a serious writer.

Artistically, Asher represented a clean break from Brian's past. As an outsider who was free of the band's internal politics, he could help extend the thoughtful songwriting that

Brian and Mike Love had begun with tunes such as "Please Let Me Wonder," "Kiss Me Baby," and "She Knows Me Too Well." While these songs proved Love's lyrical capabilities, Brian was preoccupied with keeping the music fresh. "When Brian and I first met to discuss the album, he was emphatic in telling me that he did not want to write anything like the Beach Boys had done before," Asher explains. "He also made it clear that he didn't want to work with any of the lyricists he'd previously written with.

"When we first met to talk about the album, I told Brian that I wasn't into surfing and that I didn't have a handle on the surf vernacular. Nor did I know what words would be correct for car racing songs. 'My guess is that I wouldn't be very good at writing that kind of song,' I said. Brian was very clear in his response. 'We're not going to do typical Beach Boys songs, so forget anything that comes to mind when you think of one. That's why I'm calling you. If I wanted that kind of song, there are plenty of other people who could do them.'"

To Brian, Asher was the quintessential sophisticate: he was bright, affable, and devilishly handsome. He also traveled in hip social circles, and possessed a keen sensibility and quick wit—qualities that made it difficult for anyone *not* to like him. Yet, to this day, Asher remains perplexed by Brian's invitation. "Why did Brian call me instead of someone else? I'm not really sure. Apparently, he and Loren Schwartz had a conversation in which Brian bemoaned the fact that he had to do this album [*Pet Sounds*] for Capitol, and that he was behind in the writing. The other Beach Boys were out of the country, but he didn't want to write with them anyway. Loren must have said, 'Hey, why don't you call Tony? He's a bright guy.'"

Born in London in 1939 to silent film star Laura La Plante and movie producer Irving Asher, Tony migrated to Los Angeles with his mother and sister Jill when he was less than six months old, his father staying behind in England to join the US army and fight in World War II. His family's show business roots guided his appreciation for the cultural arts, and his parents' prominence in Hollywood allowed for a privileged upbringing. La Plante, one of Universal's top silent screen stars, was best known for her roles in *Skinner's Dress Suit* (1926), *The Cat and the Canary* (1927), and *The Last Warning* (1929). Irving, who served as head of production at Warner Bros., was nominated for an Academy Award in 1941 for *Blossoms in the Dust*. The film, along with *Citizen Kane* and *The Maltese Falcon*, lost to Darryl Zanuck's *How Green Was My Valley*.

As a boy, Tony played piano and composed. In college, he gigged at nightclubs and pizza parlors around Los Angeles with a bass-playing friend, and later teamed up with songwriter Kelly Gordon, whose gritty "That's Life" became a hit for Frank Sinatra. After graduating from UCLA with a degree in journalism, Asher began his advertising career at the Carson/Roberts/Inc. agency. His timing couldn't have been better: the firm was on the brink of signing a million-dollar television deal with Mattel Toys, and Tony's musical background would be a valuable asset.

Though they hadn't been formally introduced, Wilson and Asher first crossed paths at the home of Loren Schwartz. "I thought [Tony] was a cool person," Wilson told David Leaf in 1996. "Anybody that hung out with Loren Schwartz was a very brainy guy—a real verbal person." As Asher remembers, he later bumped into Brian at Western Recorders: "In the early '60s, the Hollywood recording studios were mostly used in the evening—music people just weren't getting up until two o'clock in the afternoon. To fill the down time during the day, the studios courted the advertising agencies, because they recorded a lot of jingles. I frequently worked at Western Recorders because it wasn't far from my agency. And I liked Chuck Britz. I was at Western one day, and when I went to the water cooler in the hall, Brian was standing there. I recognized him from the parties at Loren's house, and introduced myself. 'Hi, Brian. How are you doing?' 'Great!' he said.

"Now, if I had met him on the street, or at a party, or almost anywhere else I think he would have said a very quick 'hello' and dismissed me. But because I was in a recording studio, and possibly because he made a mental connection between Loren Schwartz and me, it gave me some credibility. While I didn't pass out and fall down when I met him, I was certainly impressed. Even then I was aware that he was the real brain behind the Beach Boys. I knew he was 'The Man.'

"Earlier that day, I'd heard Brian in the studio closest to the water cooler. The door was open, and I could hear his voice coming out of the room. Now, moments after we met, he was saying, 'Come in and listen to this.' It was amazing! Brian took me into a little studio, where there were a couple of engineers and some keyboards: a regular acoustic piano, a Hammond B-3 organ, and a Fender Rhodes electric piano. We were in the booth, and he said, 'I'm putting down a couple of demos.' He directed the engineer to play what he'd recorded. I listened and said, 'That's great.' He ran out into the studio and played something on the piano; it was the countermelody he planned to layer over what we had just listened to. For years, people have asked what he played for me that day, and the truth is, I don't know. They were just fragments—works in progress.

"I was sitting with him on the piano bench, and I started playing something that I had written, and then he played something else—a different tune he was working on. We had a nice little back-and-forth thing going on. We could have gone on and on, but I had a session running in the other studio, so after about 15 minutes, I reluctantly said, 'I have to go—I have a session.' I told him my name again, and I might have given him a business card. That was it, until the day he called me to help write the album."

Lyric Musings

By the time Brian summoned Asher, he'd finished a number of melodies and had begun working on the instrumental recordings. While Brian wrote most of the album's lyrics with Asher, three of the eleven lyrical tunes on *Pet Sounds* were written with other collaborators: "I Know There's an Answer" (with Terry Sachen and Mike Love), "I'm Waiting for the Day" (with Mike Love), and "Sloop John B," a traditional folk tune that was adapted by Wilson and Al Jardine.

Unfortunately, neither Asher nor Wilson documented the exact dates of their collaboration or when they completed the lyrics to individual songs. They also neglected to save any of the music drafts produced during their daily work sessions—valuable artifacts that would have offered accurate dates and a definitive view of the creative process. As Asher remembers, he and Brian completed the lyrics to all of the *Pet Sounds* songs except for "You Still Believe in Me" before any of the instrumental tracks were recorded, but the absence of any official paperwork precludes listing composition dates— or even vocal recording session dates—with any certainty. According to the recording ledgers, most of the instrumental sessions were held between January and March, and the vocal sessions were conducted between March and April. This—along with Tony Asher's recollection that he first visited Brian at home in January—means that the bulk of the songs were likely written over a two- to three-week period between January and February 1966, and that recording began as quickly as tunes were finished.

Asher vividly remembers his first meeting with Brian, and describes how they began working on *Pet Sounds*: "It may sound surprising, but the Laurel Way house was rather unremarkable. If you walked in, you wouldn't have said, 'This is the home of a rock star.' It was located in a beautiful community; it was a nice house, with large rooms and a swimming pool. It was a regular, horizontal California-style ranch house. When you entered the front door, you came into an immense living room with a piano. The piano dominated the room: it was off to the side in a corner, but it was a major piece of furniture in the house. This was where we spent most of our time writing *Pet Sounds*. The other place we spent a lot of time was the kitchen. Brian was always hungry!

"The living room had a couple of big sofas, and there was a fireplace with an angled wall above it. On that wall was a tapestry with the image of a bird embroidered into it. One time we got really stoned and started hallucinating that the bird took flight. That's when I knew I was in trouble! Directly across the living room was a glass wall with sliding doors leading to the pool. Off to the side was a small room that Brian used as a playback studio—a room where he could play tapes from the studio. That home studio had good speakers, a four-track tape machine, and a board. The shelves were lined with boxes of tape reels.

"We didn't write anything that first day—Brian just played some stuff for me, and said, 'I've got a couple of tunes, but I don't know if I want to put them on the album or not.' One of them was 'In My Childhood,' which became 'You Still Believe in Me.' I wrote the words at home—apart from Brian—and he was very pleased with what I came up with.

"Looking back, it never occurred to me that Brian would listen to what I had written and say, 'Oh gee, this is great, thanks a lot—let me call you if I want to do some more,' or 'You know, I really don't like this.' Normally, I was a bit apprehensive whenever I presented a new commercial to my boss or a client. But that just wasn't an issue with this album, although I can't explain why.

"Brian was happy, and said, 'What kind of schedule do you want to work on?' We figured it would take a couple of solid weeks to write the album, so I went to my employer and said, 'I've got to have a two- or three-week sabbatical.' When I told my boss what was up, he was delighted for me—he recognized it as a once-in-a-lifetime opportunity.

"On a normal day I'd arrive at the house by 10:00 A.M., and Brian would wake up at 11:30. We'd get together at 12:00 noon, and he'd usually say, 'I'm hungry—let's get something to eat.' We procrastinated a lot! I got smart and stopped coming at 10:00. Some days, Brian would say, 'Let's get started early tomorrow—at 10:30.' I'd say, 'Fine,' but I would show up at noon, and he'd still be asleep. I couldn't complain: no one wants to stare at a blank piece of paper and say, 'OK, I've got to write a great song,' and that's really what we were doing. If the opportunity to talk about something other than work arose during our sessions, we would take advantage of it for the same reason—we didn't want to face the daunting task at hand.

"We always worked at the piano. Brian would sit on the bench and I'd stand next to him. He would make up melodies, which he'd sing without actually singing words. I would often have some comment about the melody, like 'Gee, I liked it better when you modulated up there instead of going down,' or 'Why don't you start with that section, and go back to the other one later in the song?' My comments stemmed from whatever my gut reaction was. Typically, Brian would respond with, 'Oh yeah—you mean go up there? OK—go up the first time, and then the second time stay down.' He'd try it that way, and say, 'Gosh—what if I did this? That would be even better!' I'd add ideas like that, and Brian almost always gave my suggestions consideration, although he didn't always end up agreeing with me.

"I'd take home what we had done during the day, and polish it at night. I'd frequently add another verse to what we'd written, and then we'd work on it again the next day after I'd played it for Brian. But we did write some 'complete' songs during our sessions together—like 'God Only Knows.' It's a short song, and I think Brian spent more time tweaking the instrumental part than we did writing the words! None of the others came that easily.

"Even though Brian wrote the melodies and I wrote the lyrics, it's difficult to say who was responsible for different parts of a song. There was a lot of give and take on both our parts. We both contributed emotion and feeling, musically and lyrically. Except for two songs ["You Still Believe In Me" and "Wouldn't It Be Nice"] it was an interactive process. He never said, 'Here's the melody, now go write the lyrics.' Brian would play the melody, and I'd find the words that had the right cadence and rhythm. If I wrote a word or a phrase that he didn't like, I would change it. Sometimes I'd ask him 'How does this sing?' and he'd sing it so I could hear how the words fit into the melody.

"I had an edge, because I could write and play music. I've worked with other songwriters who refused to change a melody once they've written it, but Brian was very flexible, and I was able to make melodic contributions. If he couldn't remember a chord change that he'd played earlier, I would remind him of it. It was fun to do that—it helped us develop a collaborative relationship, and by the time a song was finished, you couldn't even say 'Who wrote what?' But in the end, the musical inspiration was Brian's—I simply helped with the structure of the songs.

"How did Brian come up with those gorgeous melodies? It was exciting to watch him when he was on to something, because he'd become very enthusiastic. He'd run over to the piano, and begin playing a 'feel.' That's what I called it at the time too—it's the way people talked about those things. People would go to recording sessions and say, 'Did you hear that new Phil Spector song? God, isn't it a great feel—with the guitars?' It reflected the era's music vernacular.

"Along the way, he played plenty of feels that we never turned into songs. Lots of times you play a feel and think it's a song. You say, 'Hey, this is great!' You think it'll be a great song, and somehow it takes a slight turn while you're finishing it, and you follow the twist in the road. 'Yeah, that's cool, let's try that.' Sometimes, you never get back to the original idea, because the whole song has gone in a different direction. Before you know it, you've got a song—but it isn't the song you set out to write. To that extent, the *Pet Sounds* writing experience was a free-form exercise. Our working relationship was so spontaneous that when we sat down we didn't know if we were going to write a ballad or a rhythm tune, or one in a major or minor key. There wasn't any master plan.

"Because of the nature of our work, a lot of our down time was spent talking, and as digressive as those idle conversations seemed to be, they helped establish a mood. We'd usually talk about women—it's almost all we talked about other than music. I think we realized that it was the subject we ought to be talking about, because it's the kind of feeling we wanted to capture in our songs. We were young kids, but we'd had plenty of dating experience. Our hearts had been broken a few times, we'd coveted someone we couldn't have, and we'd had a girl turn out to be very different from what we thought she was going to be. Each of those things had already happened to us, so we were able to talk about those experiences in relation to the work we were doing.

"Brian would sometimes start the conversation about somebody he had known, or perhaps I would; it moved in all directions from there. We talked a lot about how certain things made us feel. 'Caroline No' is a perfect example of a song that was preceded by one of these free-flow discussions. Not that we had a conversation about a girl named Caroline who had cut her hair—I don't mean that at all. But we would get into a certain mood by virtue of having discussions that would get us into a specific mindset. We talked about how wonderful it is when you first meet a girl and she looks great, and how terrible it is when you know you'll be breaking up at any moment. Consequently, when we finally did move to the piano to start working, we'd write a song based on the sort of mood we had put each other in at that time through the discussion we'd just been having.

"I wasn't drawing exclusively on my own thoughts and emotions during this time. I talked about my relationships, and Brian talked about his. Much of what comes from this sort of creative process is sparked subconsciously, and a lot of those subconscious thoughts were ignited by the mood of a discussion that Brian and I might have had a few hours, or even the day, before. He expressed some ambivalence toward Marilyn, which was natural for someone his age. He was expressing the kinds of feeling that all young married people have: 'Should I have given up my freedom so early?' It's similar to when a psychiatrist tells you that to some extent, every character in your dreams is you.

"Quite often, we'd begin writing a song based on those discussions, and Brian would stop and say, 'Let's see where we are.' We'd back off and listen to the whole thing instead of zeroing in on a particular word or phrase. A few times, he looked at me and said, 'This is really different.' He'd suddenly be aware of how much of a departure these songs were for him."

The pair's open-minded approach allowed them to write some of the most contemplative songs of their day. Much more than just catchy tunes, these are personal statements that attached words and meaning to our most private thoughts and feelings. Bob Dylan may have written outspokenly about peace, war, and activism, but Brian Wilson and Tony Asher constructed songs that made every man's emotions accessible.

Concept Album?

The songs on *Pet Sounds* loosely chronicle the rise and fall of an adolescent relationship as viewed from the boy's perspective. The thematic unity of the tunes they wrote and the cleverness with which they framed the couple's emotions raises an important question: did Brian consciously plan for *Pet Sounds* to tell a story through its logical progression of songs? Is it a true concept album, in which every single song plays an active role in advancing the story line or idea? The songs suggest this, although Brian has never expounded on what conceptual form he may have had in mind for the album. He is often quoted as saying that *Pet Sounds* was "a heart and soul album," that "they were all inspirational songs," and that "there's a lot of love in it." While these comments bear truth, they don't explain whether he purposely set out to tell an uninterrupted story.

Although he didn't help to sequence the album, Tony Asher remembers no preconceived plan to write a "concept" album. "When we began working, Brian viewed the songs— some of them just fragments—as pieces of a puzzle. I'm sure that, even then, he had a clear idea of how he wanted the songs to take form—he just wasn't sure how he'd fit them together. One thing we did not say was, 'OK, let's look at the songs we have so far. What mood haven't we gotten to yet?' Some people have suggested that we had that in mind, and I can promise you we didn't consciously do that. We didn't say, 'Let's write a song about unrequited love,' or 'Let's write a song about a love affair that goes bad,' or 'Let's write about two young people who wish they could be together, but they can't.' We never said, 'Now we need a song that fits right in here.' It wasn't that kind of thing at all.

"Out of the eight songs we wrote, I'd say there were three where the idea and name of the song was 100 percent mine. The reason I mention that is because in those situations Brian acted as an editor. If I had come up with an idea he didn't like, he would have said so. But it wasn't as though he determined the subject matter of every song, and then had me write it. That would have been more likely if he had an overarching idea of what he wanted the album to be. In all honesty, I was not aware at any point that we were writing an album that had a beginning and an end to it. In fact, I had nothing to do with choosing the order of the songs on the record. I'm assuming that Brian himself put the songs in the order they're in, and that considerable thought went into that. I don't know if he was trying to do what some people have said the album does, or if he was simply saying, 'Gee, we need a slow tune now,' or 'I don't want to put two minor things in a row.'"

Whether *Pet Sounds* is a concept album in the strictest sense is debatable. To its credit, the record has a convincing flow, moving effortlessly from unrestrained optimism

("Wouldn't It Be Nice" and "You Still Believe in Me") to pessimistic doubt ("God Only Knows" and "Here Today"), concluding in wistful resignation ("Caroline No"). But along the way, two unrelated themes ("Sloop John B" and "Pet Sounds") intercede, upsetting the program's graceful emotional curve. Although their inclusion snaps the album's thematic thread and undermines the concept, they do contribute to the marvelous pacing of the record.

There's no denying that this array of songs, with mostly similar themes and an appreciable continuity of production, signaled a new direction for both the Beach Boys and the recording industry. With few exceptions, most rock 'n' roll albums of the day were "assembled" by adding filler tunes to a handful of the artist's hit singles. Radio's AOR (album oriented rock) format didn't yet exist, and rock groups were slow to follow the impressive concept model perfected by traditional pop artists such as Frank Sinatra and Ella Fitzgerald. By 1965 the Beatles had begun to do it, though, and, starting with *The Beach Boys Today!*, Brian Wilson began doing it too.

So is *Pet Sounds'* greatness based on its reputation as a concept album, or on the exceptional cohesiveness of melody, lyrics, performance, and production? The beauty of *Pet Sounds* is that each listener can correctly draw his or her own conclusion—which is how it ought to be.

The Songs
Viewed as a whole, *Pet Sounds* reflects an emotional journey that gently moves from the eternal optimism of a blossoming romance to the desolation of its demise. Within its songs,

Wilson and Asher boiled exhilaration, fear, love, hope, desperation, and wonder down to their cores, cramming their essences into meaning-filled vessels that open a window to Brian's soul. "The lyrics are models of perfection," says David Wild, senior editor of *Rolling Stone* magazine. "They're intelligent and moving, but they're not pretentious. The *Pet Sounds* songs have a Tin Pan Alley economy that is artful."

Wouldn't It Be Nice

"Wouldn't It Be Nice" is the perfect opener: an effervescent anthem that celebrates the anticipation of romantic freedom that every young couple yearns for. Here, they find solace in thinking and talking about getting married ("Wouldn't it be nice to live together/in the kind of world where we belong?"). Their plea is optimistic ("Maybe if we think and wish and hope and pray it might come true"), their dream filled with conviction. Although talking about that dream is frustrating, it's their only way to keep its blissful spirit alive ("You know the more we seem to talk about it/it only makes it worse to live without it—but let's talk about it").

Asher believes the lyric has a universal resonance that still expresses the longing that adolescents feel today. "It's a song that people who are young and in love can appreciate and respond to, because it revolves around the things they've always wanted to do: live together, sleep together, wake up together—do everything together. I love the fact that the song has such a nice, bouncy feel to it. When we were writing, I was aware of the intricate rhythms that Brian had accomplished musically. There are changes in tempo and legato parts that make it very interesting."

As Asher recalls, the song developed in an unusual way: "Over a period of days, Brian kept saying that he was working on a melody, but he didn't want to play it for me until he had the structure finished. One day, he said, 'It's done.' He sat at the piano and played what turned out to be 'Wouldn't It Be Nice.' He immediately said, 'Let's start writing the lyric.' I got a legal pad and a pencil and sat next to him.

"Writing 'Wouldn't It Be Nice' was different from the way we wrote the other songs for *Pet Sounds*, because once he had perfected the melody, Brian's job was finished and the focus was on me writing the lyrics. When we first attacked this song, Brian kept looking at the page to see what I had written. He'd say, 'No, no, no—I don't like that. Let's do something else.' I would write three words, and he'd make some comment about those three words. After a short time, I realized that he was microanalyzing the individual words because he had nothing else to do! I said 'Brian, let me take a tape of this home. I'll write the lyrics then come back.' Thank God he agreed, because it would have been tortuous writing the whole album under so fine a microscope.

"After breathing a sigh of relief, I went home and finished the song. There are a lot of words in 'Wouldn't It Be Nice,' and to stand there and write it one word at a time would have been crazy. After 'Wouldn't It Be Nice,' we started writing songs in a more integrated and collaborative way, developing the melody and the lyrics at the same time." (For the record, Asher wasn't the sole contributor to "Wouldn't It Be Nice." The round-robin "Good night, oh baby, Sleep tight, oh baby" coda was a catchy phrase that Mike Love developed in the studio while working through the vocal arrangement.)

You Still Believe in Me

Asher developed an acutely personal lyric that emphasized the frailty of human nature for "You Still Believe in Me," in which a boy admits he is powerless over his impulses. He understands his faults ("I try hard to be strong, but sometimes I fail myself"), and is moved by his lover's unwavering loyalty ("And after all I've done to you, how can it be you still believe in me?"). But his immaturity precludes him from acting responsibly, and instead of saying, "I'm sorry for my mistakes," he says,"I know I'm not being faithful, and I can't believe you still love me." His mournful wail (Brian's falsetto "I wanna cry") at the song's end signals a desperate plea for forgiveness. "I was able to close my eyes and go into a world and sing a little more effeminately and more sweetly—which allows a lot more love to come down through me," Brian said.

As Asher recalls, it was the first song that he and Wilson wrote for the album. "On the first day of our collaboration, Brian played me the melody for a song he'd written called 'In My Childhood.' If I remember correctly, the original melody sounded exactly the way it does on the album, and someone had already written lyrics. Brian never played me the existing lyric—he played the instrumental track and said, 'I don't even want you to hear the lyric that's been written.' He gave me a tape of the track—a cassette—and then went to the piano and made a second tape, with him playing the melody and singing dummy lyrics. I took the two cassettes from that first day home and wrote the lyric to what became known as 'You Still Believe in Me'—apart from Brian. He liked the lyric I came up with, and though we may have tinkered with a few lines here or there, it's the song you hear on the album."

That's Not Me

"That's Not Me" recounts a young man's uncertain journey toward self-discovery, and represents the struggle for independence that we all face ("I had to prove that I could make it alone now/but that's not me"). In this case, the protagonist has an ulterior motive: to impress a girl with his maturity and faithfulness ("I could try to be big in the eyes of the world/but what matters to me is what I could be to just one girl"). Although he's grappling with uncertainty, he leaves his girl and his home ("I once had a dream, so I packed up and split for the city"). After some soul-searching, he learns that being together is better than living apart ("I soon found out that my lonely life wasn't so pretty"). In the end, the guilt of leaving on awkward terms makes him fearful of returning ("I'm a little bit scared 'cause I haven't been home in a long time/You needed my love and I know that I left at the wrong time"). While not as popular as some of the other *Pet Sounds* songs, its sparse orchestration and uncommon form make "That's Not Me" one of the most appealing on the record. Lyrically, however, Asher feels he missed the mark. "I've always wished that I had the chance to go back and rewrite 'That's Not Me.' It's got nothing to do with Brian's composition; I feel that he incorporated some very interesting chord changes into his composition. But I struggled to find the right words to fit the melody—I found it very difficult to write to, and I think that comes through in the somewhat labored sound of the lyrics."

Don't Talk (Put Your Head on My Shoulder)

An aching vulnerability envelopes this song, in which Wilson and Asher confront the enigmatic power of unspoken love ("I can hear so much in your sighs/and I can see so much in your eyes"). Their goal was to communicate the couple's devotion without verbalizing it ("There are words we both could say/but don't talk, put your head on my shoulder"). As Asher explains, it was not an easy task: "It's strange to sit down and write a song about not talking. As often happened, 'Don't Talk' evolved from one of our seemingly inconsequential discussions about dating and nonverbal communication. That's a very difficult thing to translate into a song, but we managed to do it and it came off well."

From a musical perspective, "Don't Talk" is enhanced by the masterful pairing of instrumental arrangement and lyric line and—more so than any other song on *Pet Sounds*—it demonstrates Brian's exquisite use of metaphoric instrumentation. Here, the Fender bass line personifies a beating heart in the line, "Listen to my heart beat. Listen, listen, listen"— an elegant, effective touch.

I'm Waiting for the Day

Written with Mike Love, this song is a sensational reminder of the smart songs the pair wrote for *The Beach Boys Today!* In this tune, the boy falls in love with a girl who is on the rebound. She's skittish about committing to a relationship, but he pledges himself without reservation ("I guess I'm saying you're the only one/I'm waiting for the day when you can love again"). The underlying themes are commitment and strength, which Brian projects lyrically, and again, through metaphoric instrumentation.

The song begins with a heavy timpani beat, the surging percussion signaling confidence and dependability. It then shifts to a lighter beat for the bridge and the interlude, incorporating the bass flute and keyboard, gradually reintroduces weight in the interlude via a string quartet, and returns to the timpani's powerful rhythmic force for the finale. A reed instrument (possibly an oboe) suggests a sense of longing when voiced behind Brian's lead vocal ("I came along when he broke your heart"), and resignation in the final chorus ("I'm waiting for the day when you can love again"). In both cases, the instrument—and its placement—extends the unsettled feel that Wilson and Asher were aiming for.

Let's Go Away for Awhile

Two instrumental tracks on *Pet Sounds* serve as palate cleansers, offering the listener a brief respite from the program's thought-provoking vocals. The first, "Let's Go Away for Awhile," serves as a prelude to the gleaming "Sloop John B." Its detailed instrumentation affirms Brian's abilities as an orchestrator, proving that he could have easily been a successful film composer. Brian expressed affection for the song in 1967: "I think that 'Let's Go Away for Awhile' is the most satisfying piece of music I've ever made. I applied a certain set of dynamics through the arrangement and the mixing and got a full musical extension of what I'd planned during the earliest stages of the theme. I think the chord changes are very special. [I] used a lot of musicians on the track: 12 violins (I guess 'fiddles' is the hip phrase), piano, 4 saxes, oboe, vibes, and guitar with a Coke bottle on the strings for a semi-steel-guitar effect. Also, I used two basses and percussion. The total effect is 'let's go away for awhile,' which is something everyone in the world must have said at one time or other. Nice thought. Most of us don't go away, but it's still a nice thought. The track was supposed to be the backing for a vocal, but I decided to leave it alone."

Instrumental songs such as this let us hear how other composers and arrangers of the '60s affected Brian. "If you want to know the truth, I think Burt Bacharach influenced me a little bit with that ['Let's Go Away for Awhile']," he told David Leaf in 1996. "If you really analyze it and you think about it, there were a lot of chord changes similar to the way he would put something together. I think that his music had such a profound thing on my head—he got me going in a direction. I'm definitely proud of that tune."

Sloop John B

The first single from *Pet Sounds* to hit the charts owes its existence to Al Jardine's love for the Kingston Trio. "Sloop John B" has origins dating to 1926, and the excavation of the *John B* off the coast of Nassau, Bahamas. The shipwreck's story was set to a Bahamian sea chantey: a folk song lamenting the seafarer's lot. The ditty was extremely popular, prompting poet Carl Sandburg to observe that, "Time and usage have given the song the dignity of a national anthem around Nassau." Sandburg was intrigued by a 1926 arrangement by Alfred George Wathall (a Northwestern University music professor), and published the tune in his 1927 book, *The American Songbag*. The earliest recording was made in 1935, when folk music historian Alan Lomax recorded a Bahamian rhyming group singing "Histe up the John B Sail." The song was revived in 1955 by the Weavers, and received prominent attention on the Kingston Trio's 1958 debut album *The*

Kingston Trio. Thanks to Jardine, the song's greatest due came with the sparkling Beach Boys rendition featured on *Pet Sounds*. "I had a group in high school called the Islanders, and we sang 'Sloop John B' all the time. I'd been fooling around with the song at home, and thought it might be something that would work for the Beach Boys. But, it took me quite some time to convince Brian of the song's possibilities.

"We were recording at Western one afternoon, and Brian was at the piano. I said, 'I think you should hear this—I've got an idea for an arrangement that might really be interesting.' I played it. Brian wasn't into folk music, and said, 'I'm not a big fan of the Kingston Trio.' But I didn't give up on the idea. I played it for him again, this time in the Beach Boys idiom. I figured if I gave it to him in the right light, he might end up believing in it. Basically, it's a three-chord song, and I added some minor chord changes, which stretched out the possibilities from a vocal point of view. I walked away from the piano; Brian digested it, and we went back to work.

"The next day, I got a call to come down to the studio. Brian played the song for me, and I was blown away. From idea stage to the completed [instrumental] track took less than 24 hours. Brian had never shown the slightest interest in folk music, but he was certainly passionate about this song, and his interest manifested itself in a beautiful production.

"The song's original lyrics are unusual. They don't have meaning in the lyrical sense now—they're from another era. They're archaic English, and we had to change one of the words. In one line we sing, 'I feel so broke up . . . .' The original translation from Sandburg was, 'I feel so break up.' There are some chord progressions in our version that give the song a different expression—a 'Beach Boys' expression. It makes the singing a lot more interesting. Overall, it has a John Philip Sousa dimension to it."

Although the record became an instant classic, Jardine feels he never received adequate credit: "When I brought 'Sloop John B' to Brian, I was terrified. I thought I might be wasting his time. Not so—I gave him the chords, and he soaked them up like a sponge. He made the instrumental track almost immediately, and it became a huge hit for us. But he never acknowledged my contribution to the song."

There's no questioning the importance of "Sloop John B" in the Beach Boys canon: it features some of the group's most complicated and breathtaking vocal harmonies, and it displays the best of Brian's meticulous production skills. But does it really belong on *Pet Sounds*? Does it fit alongside the record's highly personalized tunes? In this writer's opinion it doesn't, because it interrupts the program's pleasurable flow and destroys the notion of *Pet Sounds* as a bona-fide concept album.

The song was included on the album at the suggestion of Capitol Records. "'Sloop John B' was important to Capitol— it meant they had a hit single on *Pet Sounds*," Jardine explained. "We were not predisposed to give them 'Good Vibrations,' which was a big mistake. Brian was insistent that we hold it ['Good Vibrations'], and Capitol said, 'we need a single. How are we going to sell this thing?'"

Given the time, effort, and care he devoted to the album's creation, it's surprising that Brian would defer to the label's poor judgment. How could he have let this spectacular but inappropriate selection mar his nearly perfect tone poem? In truth, Brian may not have seen it as an issue. The basic track was recorded on July 12, 1965—six months before the first *Pet Sounds* recording session. Its final overdubs were completed in December. Tony Asher remembers it as being the only finished tune that Brian played for him at their first meeting in January 1966, which raises the possibility that Brian may *not* have objected to including it on the album—meaning that he wasn't necessarily tied to the concept of a *concept*.

Regardless of Brian's intention, or where each listener stands on the merits of its inclusion, "Sloop John B"— released two months before *Pet Sounds* and the first song on the album to hit *Billboard*'s Top 10—remains a stimulating, controversial part of the *Pet Sounds* saga.

God Only Knows

While "Sloop John B" could be considered *Pet Sounds'* conceptual nadir, "God Only Knows" is its goodwill ambassador: a well-placed exclamation point that punctuates the album's spiritual sonority. It comes at a critical juncture in the program, serving as the pivot point on which the album hinges. It is considered to be the Beach Boys' finest record, and with it Wilson and Asher reached their zenith, creating an essential work of art that might just be the most inspiring song in all of rock 'n' roll music. It is also the favorite of many songwriters, including Paul McCartney and Jimmy Webb. "I love 'God Only Knows' and its bow to the baroque that goes all the way back to 1740 and J. S. Bach," Webb says. "It represents the whole tradition of liturgical music that I feel is a spiritual part of Brian's music. And Carl's singing is pretty much at its pinnacle—as good as it ever got."

Both musically and technically, "God Only Knows" marks a true departure for Brian and the Beach Boys. Brian never duplicated the wondrous feats accomplished with the writing, performance, and production of this awe-inspiring recording.

What is it that sets "God Only Knows" apart? Firstly, there's the song's composition. In structuring his tunes, Brian often modified the popular 32-bar A-A-B-A song pattern to suit his needs. On "God Only Knows" he added a contrasting vocal interlude to the bridge and a round-style vocal tag to the ending. On their own, these devices were rather ordinary, but in this song, Brian uses the breaks to highlight some spectacular vocal harmony effects, which augment the tune's rarefied tone.

The unconventional vocal embellishments integrated into the arrangement (for example, the complicated in-and-out vocal round at the song's end) were far more sophisticated than anything the Beach Boys—or any other modern pop vocal group—had done before. There is also a fine interplay between the vocal and melodic portions of the song; a subtle musical contrast that tempers the tune's celebratory melody with the bittersweet irony of its lyrics—an effect that appreciably strengthens the song's emotional impact.

Moreover, who would have guessed from its title that "God Only Knows" has nothing to do with God, but everything to do with teenage angst? Few songwriters of the day dared to write secular pop tunes featuring "God" in the title. Tony Asher recalls that he and Brian had strong reservations about the word, and grappled with the decision to use it: "We had lengthy conversations during the writing of 'God Only

Knows,' because unless you were Kate Smith and you were singing 'God Bless America,' no one thought you could say 'God' in a song. No one had done it, and Brian didn't want to be the first person to try it. He said, 'We'll just never get any air play.' Isn't it amazing that we thought that? But it worked, and 'God Only Knows' is, to me, one of the great songs of our time. I mean *the* great songs. Not because I wrote the lyrics, but because it is an amazing piece of music that we were able to write a very compelling lyric to. It's the simplicity—the inference that 'I am who I am because of you'—that makes it very personal and tender.

"This is the one that I thought would be a hit record, because it was so incredibly beautiful. I was concerned that maybe the lyrics weren't up to the same level as the music: how many love songs start off with the line, 'I may not always love you'? I liked that twist, and fought to start the song that way. Working with Brian, I didn't have a whole lot of fighting to do, but I was certainly willing to fight to the end for that. I was probably saying to myself, 'God, I hope I'm right about this,' because you're never quite sure. But I knew that it would work, because by the second part, the real meaning of the song has come out: 'I'll love you till the sun burns out, then I'm gone,' ergo 'I'm gonna love you forever.' I guess that in the end, 'God Only Knows' is the song that most people remember, and love the most."

One can appreciate Asher's concern, given the song's many contradictions. Of all the songs written for *Pet Sounds*, "God Only Knows" is the one most open to wide lyrical interpretation—the song that best emphasizes the subjective and often prickly nature of lyrical analysis. Clearly, the song's protagonist is expressing his gratitude for his girlfriend's love, and cannot contemplate a world without her ("I may not always love you/but long as there are stars above you/you never need to doubt it.") The character's thoughts are based in the present, and if viewed solely from this perspective, the song is eternally optimistic.

However, the following lines, "If you should ever leave me/though life would still go on, believe me/the world could show nothing to me/so what good would living do me?" suggest a greater complexity. Although one could reasonably conclude that the central character is asserting that if the couple's love dies, *he* will die, within his declaration of unconditional love lies a daunting subtext: "I love you now, but if we ever part, life will go on. I will survive in spite of you."

It could be argued that with the line "I may not always love you" the protagonist subconsciously anticipates a time when he and his girl will no longer be together. Whose life is the character referring to when he sings, " . . .life would still go on, believe me?" Is he saying, "I won't stop living because you left me—believe me, I won't"? In one breath he sounds defensive, but in the next, he asks himself the rhetorical question "what good would living do me?" How and why will the character's life go on? It's a doom-laden prospect—one that is at odds with both the song's upbeat tempo and the seemingly happy tone set by the grouping of tunes on the first half of the album.

More questions abound. Is the boy in the song Brian's alter ego? More than with any other composition on *Pet Sounds* (except, perhaps "I Just Wasn't Made For These Times"), we can draw a direct line between Brian's personal life and the song's protagonist. The overwhelming message is that the character lacks confidence: in himself, in his girl, and in the stability of their relationship. By his own admission, Brian's relationship with Marilyn was, at the time, tenuous. And his drug use—a byproduct of insecurity—could easily have spawned the paranoid thoughts pervading the song's underlying theme.

We can also read into Brian's selection of Carl to sing the lead. At first, it was Brian who sang lead. After hearing a rough mix of the record, however, Brian decided that Carl's voice was better suited for the reverential tone he desired. Did the lyric cut too close to the bone for Brian to go on record singing the song himself?

While these questions may never be answered, one fact remains: "God Only Knows" reflects everything in Brian's music that makes us feel good. "I was really grateful to be the one to sing that song," Carl Wilson once said. "It is so beautifully written, it sings itself."

I Know There's an Answer

As his work with Brian progressed, Tony Asher learned that he wasn't the only lyricist writing songs for *Pet Sounds*:

"Brian startled me one afternoon by saying, 'Oh, listen—I just wrote a song with Terry [Sachen, the band's road manager].' I listened to it and said to myself, 'You mean I'm not writing all the songs for the album?' I was kind of surprised—I didn't know that he was writing with anyone else. Then I got a grip on reality and thought, 'He doesn't have any obligation to write anything with me, let alone the whole album.' I didn't feel betrayed—I was just surprised."

"I Know There's an Answer" (written with Terry Sachen and Mike Love) was originally called "Hang On to Your Ego." Its message, which implored users to be cautious of LSD's mind-blowing effects, was a sore point that offended Mike Love. He protested and, as he explains, insisted on a revision: "'Hang On to Your Ego' was too much of a doper song to me. My mindset at the time (not having done LSD, heroin, or cocaine) was that we shouldn't be promoting that stuff, so in a sense, I was being the straight guy in the group—the square. The people that I'd seen indulge in those things exhibited behaviors and mannerisms that left much to be desired, and 'Hang On to Your Ego' was a lyrical byproduct of that drug subculture. I thought a positive message that wasn't related to the drug culture would be preferable on *Pet Sounds*, so I came up with the alternative lyric, which reflected finding yourself.

"I always tried to put a positive spin on things. Astrologically, Brian is a Gemini, and they write through desperation. I'm a Pisces, and I write through inspiration. It's a different way of coming at it. I suggested another direction to go in, and Brian didn't balk. Maybe he cared, maybe he didn't. He never said anything to me directly."

A recording session on February 9, 1966, yielded the song's instrumental backing track, which was slated on the session tape (and listed on musician union contracts) as "Let Go of Your Ego." One week later, a vocal overdub was made and the tune was renamed "Hang On to Your Ego." Retaining the original instrumental track of February 9, the group later redubbed the vocal with Mike's revised lyrics, calling the song "I Know There's an Answer."

In reality, the lyric changes were negligible. Except for eliminating the veiled reference to the ego-shattering effects of the drug, the lyrics aren't radically different. Ironically, the refrain containing the most blatant nod to LSD ("They come on like they're peaceful but inside they're so uptight/They trip through the day and waste all their thoughts at night,") remains identical in both versions.

Compositionally, "I Know There's an Answer" is intriguing. The song follows a verse/refrain/verse/refrain/bridge/refrain pattern, with an instrumental solo on the final refrain. The verse is actually split into two parts: an eight-bar "A" section ("I know so many people"), and a six-bar "B" section ("I know there's an answer"). The coupling of an eight- and a six-bar passage to create a fourteen-bar verse is rare (most verses are eight, twelve, or sixteen bars long); in this case, the listener isn't aware of the verse's compositional irregularity because the tune is so well written.

Here Today

A stark reminder that feelings can change on a whim ("Love is here today and it's gone tomorrow/it's here and gone so fast"), "Here Today" is an admonishment to approach new relationships with caution ("A brand new love affair is such a beautiful thing/but if you're not careful think about the pain it can bring"). The words reflect the perspective of "the other guy," who is telling his ex-lover's new boyfriend to be circumspect because of his own experience with the girl ("Well you know I hate to be a downer/but I'm the guy she left before you found her"). Like "God Only Knows," the lyric reveals a palpable defensiveness ("She made me feel so bad, she made my heart feel sad, she made my days go wrong, and made my nights so long").

The song also has an odd construction that, according to Asher, made it difficult to write: "I wrote more lyrics to 'Here Today' than we used. The song has several sections that vary in tempo, and Brian and I struggled to find a lyric that we were both happy with." Here, Brian used the verse/chorus/verse/chorus pattern, but the allocation of measures within each section is atypical of most pop music—or any music, for that matter. The first two verses are almost identical: both are 20 bars long, and each contains three sections with unusual bar structures (section one is eight bars, section two is seven bars, and section three is five bars in length). A three-section, 20-bar break (eight, six, and six bars, respectively) separates the second and third chorus.

While it is rare for a chorus to contain an odd number of measures, all three choruses on "Here Today" are seven bars. Most choruses are eight bars long. Occasionally a chorus will be *lengthened* to imply suspense or extension of time. The purposeful *shortening* of the choruses here emphasizes the "here today, gone tomorrow" idea reflected in the lyric.

I Just Wasn't Made for These Times

Perhaps the most sensitive, moving song on *Pet Sounds*, "I Just Wasn't Made For These Times" is a plaintive ballad about coming to terms with one's differences ("I keep looking for a place to fit in where I can speak my mind"). Throughout, questions are raised: Why am I always making mistakes? ("They say I got brains, but they ain't doing me no good/I wish they could/Each time things start to happen again, I think I

got something good going for myself/but what goes wrong?")
Who can I trust? ("Where can I turn when my fair-weather
friends cop out?") The protagonist is desperate to define himself, but is depressed and struggling. Ultimately, the answer to
the question—"Where do I fit in?"—lies in the realization that
he *doesn't* ("I guess I just wasn't made for these times").

There's an overwhelming sense that the lyric represents
Brian's life, his view of himself, and his music. As Asher
remembers, Brian's feelings played a major role in the development of the lyrics: "I think that 'I Just Wasn't Made for These
Times' was Brian's way of acknowledging that he didn't
conform to the norm—that he was marching to the beat of a
different drummer. We were certainly aware of what we were
writing about when we approached this song. It was definitely
a lyric written from Brian's perspective, although during the
hours we spent writing, we didn't talk about his socialization
per se. He never asked me to interpret his feelings in one of
our songs, and certainly not this one.

"Brian never said to me, 'Man, I remember feeling left out
as a kid,' or 'I don't feel comfortable in a crowd,' although you
sometimes got the impression that that is what he might have
been feeling. We confined our conversations to the theoretical.
'What if we write about a kid somewhere who doesn't fit in?'
Many times, when we were having idle conversations, Brian
would express a feeling or emotion he felt for the song.
I would often agree, saying 'Oh yeah, I've had those feelings,
I understand.' But in this case, I couldn't relate to the feeling
of not fitting in.

"I remember that when we finished this song, I had the
sense that it might not end up on the album. It takes a lot of

courage for an artist to expose himself in such a personal way; lots of times, you question why you're doing something, or whether it's any good. I thought that maybe Brian would not want to make such a raw, emotional public statement. But he did, and it took a lot of guts."

Brian once explained the self-exploratory implication of the song, relating it directly to his work on the album. "It's about a guy who was crying because he thought he was too advanced, and that he'd eventually have to leave people behind," he explained. "All my friends thought I was crazy to do *Pet Sounds*."

Pet Sounds

Of the album's two instrumentals, "Pet Sounds" is the least fitting. Curiously sandwiched between a pair of sumptuous ballads ("I Just Wasn't Made for These Times" and "Caroline No"), the stylized tempo arrangement is jarringly out of place, and, like "Sloop John B," it bears no thematic relevance to the balance of songs. That said, "Pet Sounds" neatly ties together all of the instrumental elements that make the album a marvel. From its sensual Latin percussion (courtesy of a guiro and bongos) to the steely edginess of a heavily reverbed electric guitar, the tune is texture personified: a two-and-a-half minute rendezvous to a tropical paradise.

The song began as "Run James Run," and, along with "Trombone Dixie," was recorded just before the *Pet Sounds* sessions in November 1965. As with "Let's Go Away for Awhile," the melody has a cinematic feel that Brian purposely strove for. "['Pet Sounds'] was supposed to be a James Bond type of song," he said in 1996. "We were gonna try to get it to the James Bond people. But we thought it would never happen, so we put it on the album."

"Pet Sounds" is all about color: a fiery fantasia redolent with the jungle-like rhythm of the 1956 Les Baxter-Martin Denny hit "Quiet Village." Brian's penchant for instrumental shading and nuance clearly stems from his love for the bachelor-pad music created by Baxter and Denny, two prominent composer-arrangers of the 1950s.

Denny studied orchestration under composer Arthur Lange, a proponent of synesthesia, a mixing of the senses in which sounds are directly related to colors. Although true synesthesia (a neuropsychological phenomenon) is rare, the composer believed that color could be interpreted through music. "Lange analogized that the spectrum of colors could be compared to music," Denny told writer RJ Smith. "A darker blue would, say, be flutes, and it would go all the way up to oranges and reds and yellows and white—up the scale to trumpets. Certain instruments adapt themselves to the darker colors—purple or magenta could be a bass or a tuba."

In addition to its rainbow of colors, "Pet Sounds" contains an abundance of peculiar textures that blend familiar and unfamiliar sounds. A generous gloss of reverb adds to the ambience, although it isn't intrusive enough to disturb the essence of the tune's dynamic instrumentation.

Caroline No

There's a graceful eloquence to "Caroline No," a beguiling, melancholic tone poem that neatly summarizes the ephemeral nature of youth and love. With it, *Pet Sounds* ends as it began: with a question. In the song, Wilson and Asher condense a life of regret into two minutes of sweet, unadorned melancholy. A man looks at an aging former love ("Where did your long hair go?/Where is the girl I used to know?/ How could you lose that happy glow?"), and wonders whether they could recapture the innocence of their youth ("Could I ever find in you again/the things that made me love you so much then?/Could we ever bring 'em back once they have gone?").

As with "God Only Knows," the song's lyrical message is oblique. In classical music, dynamics, tempo, and orchestral color are used to help the listener visualize and relate the music to specific stories. Here, too, the melodic structure of the song helps us create a scenario in our mind—we can easily imagine what the character is thinking even though it's not articulated lyrically.

"Caroline No" summarizes the thoughts that have crossed the minds of many lovers: What would I do if I suddenly ran into my high school sweetheart? How would he or she look? Could we possibly rekindle our romance? Here, the character looks back with fondness on the relationship he shared with his childhood sweetheart and contemplates what might have been.

The question "Caroline, why?" leads us to believe that he's not sure *why* the relationship ended. Perhaps the protagonist's girlfriend left him without explanation, and seeing her again prompts him to question what went wrong. He doesn't blame her, but he muses and frets over a flood of unanswered questions—all unspoken, yet candidly communicated via the tune's melodic solemnity. Ultimately, the character realizes that nothing can turn back the hands of time, and Brian answers the question "could we ever bring 'em back once they have gone?" in the form of a heartrending wail at the song's end. It is, as one might expect, a resounding "Oh, Caroline, no."

In plotting "Caroline No" Brian again turned inward for inspiration. Tony Asher says that he was specific in articulating his vision for the song: "While we were toiling away on 'Caroline No,' Brian expressed a desire to go back to simpler days. Perhaps that's what we discussed and expressed here metaphorically. At that point, he was under a tremendous amount of pressure, and yearned for a time when he wasn't shouldering all the weight of the band.

"Was there a Caroline who may have inspired the song? Well, not exactly. I had broken up with my high school girlfriend, a dancer who'd moved to New York looking to make a break on Broadway. When I went east to visit her a short time later, I found that she had made some radical changes. Her name, incidentally, was Carol. And, yes—she had cut her hair. But what I saw went deeper than the cosmetic changes. She'd become a far more worldly person—it was clear that New York had caused her to grow up, and fast.

"When I first sang the lyric to Brian, I sang, 'Oh, Carol, I know.' I envisioned a song in which the girl had undergone these changes (as I had seen in my Carol) and was attempting to explain to her former lover the inevitability of growing up. My intent was to have him 'answer' her with the line, 'Oh, Carol, I know.' The purpose was to acknowledge the inevitable growth, and for him to articulate that he missed the 'old' her. Brian heard it as 'Caroline No,' which to me was a much stronger and more interesting line than the one I had in mind.

"I never thought of this as a Beach Boys song, because Brian played it at the piano and sang his own part. When he played the other songs at the piano, he would play the parts that the other guys would eventually sing. That didn't happen with 'Caroline No.' At first, I didn't think it was on the same level as the other songs we were doing, although I liked it well enough. It just didn't have the level of sophistication that the other songs had."

Brian counts "Caroline No" among his favorites. "It's a very, very big ballad; that song was probably the best I've ever written," he said in 1995. "['Caroline No'] is a story about how, once you've fucked up or once you've run your gamut with a chick, there's no way to get it back. It takes a lot of courage to do that sometimes in your life. It's a pretty love song about how this guy and this girl lost it and there's no way to get it back. I just felt sad, so I wrote a sad song."

THE SONG THAT DIDN'T MAKE IT

Before they completed their work, Wilson and Asher toyed with the idea of adding lyrics to several songs that Brian had written before beginning *Pet Sounds*. One of them was "Good Vibrations," a song that Brian worked on tirelessly during the final sessions for the album.

As Asher recalls, "I knew that Brian was looking to compress the amount of time it took to get the album done, because he was getting calls from Capitol. He might have been looking for ways to use something that had already been written. We listened to some of those things, but realized that they weren't the right kind of songs. That's how 'Good Vibrations' came about.

"Over the course of the three or four weeks we were writing *Pet Sounds*, Brian played for me a bunch of chords that would become 'Good Vibrations.' He didn't have a title for it, but he told me the story of when his mother had taken him somewhere as a kid, and a dog began barking at him. Brian jumped back and grabbed her leg. His mom said, 'Don't act like you're scared, because they can pick up the vibes.'

"Brian said, 'You know, Tony, I love the idea of being able to pick up someone else's vibes. I always thought there would be a song in that.' I agreed, and wrote a lyric to 'Good Vibrations'—not the whole tune, but an opening section. At the time, it was one of several songs that we had in the works. Since we were doing so much, it just laid there and we moved on to some other tunes. We never got back to it, and he ended up using the lyrics that Mike Love later wrote.

"I don't recall him specifically saying that he planned to put 'Good Vibrations' on *Pet Sounds*, but we had a lot of unfinished songs, and I just assumed that we would keep writing until all of those songs were finished. We never got back to 'Good Vibrations,' and suddenly, I was aware that he was putting the album together, and that we hadn't completed the song."

Was Brian planning to include "Good Vibrations" on *Pet Sounds*? At the time, all of the Beach Boys begged him to do so. In truth, the song is no more germane to the concept than "Sloop John B," although Bruce Johnston feels that the inclusion of "Good Vibrations" would have made *Pet Sounds* the commercial equivalent of the Beatles' *Sgt. Pepper's Lonely Heart's Club Band*.

"I think 'Sloop John B' is a fantastic production, but in hindsight, it probably doesn't fit on that album," says Al Jardine. "Like everyone else, I had lobbied to put 'Good Vibrations' on *Pet Sounds*, but it wasn't to be. Brian was absolutely against putting it on the album. He had the say because he was the producer, and we respected his opinion, although we didn't agree with him. We felt a bird in the hand was worth two in the bush, and knew that leaving it off the album was a mistake. As it turned out, we were right. If we'd included 'Good Vibrations,' *Pet Sounds* would have been a milestone for us."

Once the songs were finished, Brian focused on completing the recordings, while Asher returned to his job at Carson-Roberts. The lyricist recently characterized his weeks working on *Pet Sounds* as "one of the true highlights" of his life. "For me, the whole experience was almost dreamlike," he said. Unfortunately, he didn't have the chance to witness Brian polishing their words and music in the recording studio. "Brian was spending more time in the studio, so we were getting together less often. I went to a few sessions, mostly string overdub dates. Brian would call me when he wanted me to hear something, but I was working and needed to refocus on my job. Except for those few sessions, I didn't hear the album until it was done."

the making of
pet sounds

"Only passions, great passions, can elevate
the soul to great things."

Diderot

"I don't care who watches me [in the studio]. I don't do
anything that anyone else couldn't do. I use equipment
that's available to everyone—I have no secret weapon."

Brian Wilson

Although the songs provided the foundation, Brian's impeccable control is what made *Pet Sounds* a masterpiece. From conception and composition to arranging and recording, he painstakingly directed every phase of the album's production. "*Pet Sounds* wasn't the first time that one guy did everything musical on a record," says record producer Bob Irwin, a 1960s pop music expert. "But *Pet Sounds* represents the first time that an artist of Brian's stature did everything. I can't think of anyone else who brought everything together the way Brian did—at least not on the level of that record."

While artists as diverse as Les Paul, Peggy Lee, Frank Sinatra, Buddy Holly, and Bob Dylan often effectively functioned as their own producers, Brian redefined the role. His authoritative approach to recording affected many of his contemporaries. "As far as a major, modern producer who was working right in the middle of the pop milieu, no one was doing what Brian was doing," says Jimmy Webb. "We didn't even know that it was possible until he did it."

The Producer

What makes for a successful record producer? How did Brian Wilson's work in the studio affect the making of *Pet Sounds*? The recollections of participating musicians and unedited tapes from the March 10, 1966, instrumental session for "God Only Knows" at Western Studio 3 illustrate Brian's skill, and help demystify the process.

The atmosphere in the studio is busy but orderly: a cacophony of instruments tuning up, small talk, and banter between the musicians and Brian, who is in the recording booth. It is 11:00 P.M. and the players joke good-naturedly that it will be daylight before the track is cut. At the board is Chuck Britz, who tweaks the sound coming from the musicians on the other side of the glass. Blue smoke curls lazily from his ever-present cigarette; empty eggnog cartons strewn about the console attest to his client's insatiable appetite.

The musicians clustered around the microphones have been toiling for hours, learning their parts note by note. Brian, doubling as arranger and producer, coaches the musicians from the control room. He urges them along, working relentlessly to draw the exact sound he desires from each instrument. He is patient but firm, and though an occasional joke is cracked, levity is kept to a minimum. Concentration is critical, and the musicians, who are accustomed to working for the best and the worst, know they're working for one of the best tonight.

Recording Brian's tunes isn't easy. The melodies aren't familiar, and in some cases the songs haven't even been named yet. Unlike the record, film, and TV recording sessions these pros attend by day, this gig is not scripted and the music paper before them is blank. Instead of providing written charts, Wilson—an arranger of no formal training—hums and sings the ideas spiraling in his brain to his players. He gestures enthusiastically as the musicians experiment and hurriedly transcribe chord symbols onto their charts. The ten men and one woman performing in tonight's session have the finest chops on the West Coast. Around Hollywood they're known as the 'A' team, and they are revered for their fierce record of hit-making tracks.

One by one, visitors straggle in. Marilyn, the producer's wife, is in the booth with her older sister, music contractor Diane Rovell. Bruce Johnston, the youngest Beach Boy of all, arrives from the Luau in Beverly Hills, a curvaceous beauty draped on his arm. For Johnston (the band's newest member), tonight's session will be a revelation. Despite the vocalist's presence, this is not a night for singing. The breezy vocals, flowing like silken hair on an angel's head, will come later.

The players settle in, preparing to record a preliminary run-through. All of the instruments—rhythm, brass, strings, flutes, and percussion—will be recorded together, "live-to-tape." Because the first few seconds are essential to a pop song's success, Brian has spent extra time rehearsing the introduction.

There is a hasty call to order, then an authoritative "Roll tape." With eight sharp snaps of his sticks, drummer Hal Blaine delineates the meter:

Click . . . click . . . click . . . click . . . click . . . click . . . click . . . click . . .

Between the last click and the first note, there is a brief rush of silence. Then, one beat later, a cascade of happy, soulful chords spill forth from the French horn, harpsichord, and basses, spreading rays of musical sunshine through the studio. Two accordions and a set of sleigh bells chime in, adding an irresistible cheerfulness to the opening. The feel is uplifting— damn near heavenly—and as the melody unfolds, an emotional undercurrent envelops the room. As the reels of tape preserving the music whirl away behind him, Chuck Britz nods in approval. His understated affirmation says it all: "Nice, Brian—nice."

It is this moment that galvanizes the assembly. Something special is happening in this room, and everyone knows it. Working from the control booth, Brian continues the pre-take rehearsals. "Let's go—somebody count it."

The players begin again, this time missing their entrance. Brian issues a crisp edict: "No, we didn't start right—someone count it again."

The tune begins a second time, and a third, and a fourth—eleven times in all before the first real "take" is laid down. Along the way, Brian questions, chides, and instructs. There are more starts and stops, and more booth-to-studio conferences as Brian tests and tightens individual passages. When he's satisfied that everything is just right, he issues a proclamation: "This will be Take One—'God Only Knows.'"

22 takes later, he beams, satisfied that he's wrung every bit of instrumental nuance out of both the melody and the players performing it. The tape is rewound so the playback can be heard. Brian positions himself insanely close to the monitor.

Watching Brian study a playback is a curious sight. He cocks his head to one side, focusing on the massive sound blaring from the speaker just an inch or two from his ear. He leans forward, straining to hear sounds outside the range of hearing—as if being closer to the source will magically transport him inside the music. When it's over, his relief is palpable. For Brian Wilson, the process of making records seems virtually orgasmic.

It is through his records that we glimpse the real Brian Wilson: an intense perfectionist whose proclivity for introspection is rivaled only by his passion for music. "For me, making music has always been a very spiritual thing," he wrote in 1999. "I think anybody who produces records has to feel that, at least a little bit. Producing a record—the idea of taking a song, envisioning the overall sound in my head, and then bringing the arrangement to life in the studio—well, that gives me satisfaction like nothing else. And I still get quite a charge seeing my name on a record: 'Produced by Brian Wilson.'"

From the beginning, Brian relished producing his own music in the recording studio, and he did it with a daring verve that few others could match. "Brian was a dangerous producer," explained Capitol Records producer Nik Venet in an interview with David Leaf. "Dangerous in the sense that he entered and explored non-defined recording territory without a net. He was abstract when the record company wanted simple and silly. He concentrated on what could be left out as much as what would be left in."

His propensity for perfection was constant: Brian never stopped obsessing over the quality of his recordings, refusing to compromise his high standards or take the process of making records for granted. "Brian has made musical and technical contributions that inspired us all," says Phil Ramone. "He made sure the music was well recorded, well mixed, and well mastered. At that time, you couldn't make a 45 or LP sound as good as it did in the studio. But Brian always got a big, bombastic sound, as though he had no limitations. That attitude really opened the door for all producers."

As a producer, Brian was intuitive, and he understood how to temper musical expression with commercial appeal. "[I learned] how to conceive of a framework of a song, to think in terms of production, rather than just songwriting," he once explained. "I was unable to really think as a producer up until the time where I got familiar with Phil Spector's work. Then I started to see the point of making records. You're in the business to create a record, so you design the experience to be a record rather than just a song. It's good to take a good song and just work with it. But it's that record that counts. It's the record that people listen to. It's the overall sound, what they're going to hear and experience in two and a half minutes that counts."

The Spector Factor

Brian learned a great deal from Spector, one of rock's most influential figures. He was drawn to him from the moment he heard the producer's 1963 Ronettes classic "Be My Baby." "My personal hero is Phil Spector," Brian recently told Dave di Martino of *Mojo* magazine. "The power in his music was awesome. He had a huge influence on my own music—he taught me how to produce records. He taught me how to get the best sound you can get, and he taught me about drumming and echo chambers, everything."

In developing his own style, Brian strove to emulate his mentor, and vowed to surpass Spector's supreme efforts. "When Brian came into the studio, you could tell he just adored Phil—he was his idol," says Larry Levine, who was the recording engineer for almost all of Spector's record dates. "When he came to Phil's sessions he would ask questions, but Brian always understood what was happening in the studio. They had a good rapport. Phil was a champion of deserving people, and he loved what Brian was doing. I think Brian was thrilled—like we all were—with the music that was coming out of Phil. It was a tremendous thing."

Connecting with Phil Spector was a defining moment for Brian—one that had enormous bearing on his perspective and his ability to create *Pet Sounds*. The ornery Spector was generous with his pupil, allowing him to sit in on his Gold Star sessions. He also supported Brian by lambasting Nik Venet for taking undeserved credit on the early Beach Boys records. In this way, Spector motivated Brian to fight for the control he'd earned. "Phil would often run off on a diatribe about Capitol not making Brian the producer," says Levine. "He felt that Brian deserved all of the credit, all of the money, and every bit of recognition that went along with producing his own records. He would say, 'Nik has no right—Brian is the one doing all of these great things.'"

Although Venet is credited with producing the first two Beach Boys albums, he was not making the musical and technical decisions shaping the sound of the records. "Brian was really the one making the records," Carl Wilson explained to Geoffrey Himes in 1983. "Nik would call out the take numbers, but he wasn't part of making the music."

Venet (who spent considerable time working alongside him) viewed Brian as the director, and he took a back seat in the studio. "Brian [worked] as I imagine Orson Welles must have [worked] when he directed and performed in his early films," he told David Leaf. "Brian would lean over the seated engineers' shoulders, mumbling mix instructions as if the tracks would never have a chance to be remixed again. He orchestrated and arranged sections of songs out of sequence, confounding [me], the mixers, and every musician in the studio. The engineers would look at me, and I would look at them and say, 'Just stay with him, please.' I had no idea where he was going with the music either, but I would plead with them to 'stay with him.'"

Venet's role in lobbying for the band and securing their contract with Capitol Records is undeniable, as was his personal and professional love for Brian. But an ear for talent does not a producer make, and Brian quickly tired of his record label's bureaucracy. "With an artist recording in house, it's easy for people to walk in and out and destroy the process that gets you going," said Chuck Britz. "If you're in a groove, there's nothing worse than somebody coming in and asking a political or financial question."

Bucking the Trend

Shortly after recording their second album (*Surfin' USA*), Brian insisted on taking control of production. "When Brian said he wouldn't work with Nik anymore, Capitol sent over this other guy," explains Al Jardine. "Brian said, 'Look, I'm not cutting with these guys, and what's more, I'm not going to use your studio. We'll send you the next record.'"

This refusal to use Capitol's studios threw the company's execs into a tailspin and initiated a change in the traditional relationship between artists and their record labels. The group's strong sales figures forced the label to allow Brian to produce the Beach Boys' records elsewhere, a concession practically unheard of at the time. "[It was] a big thing in those days, because record companies were used to having absolute control over their artists," explained Carl Wilson. "It was especially nervy, because Brian was a 21-year-old kid with just two albums. It was unheard of. But what could they say? So we recorded at Western Recorders, which was really our home."

Like Spector, Brian preferred to record his music and vocal tracks separately, and *Pet Sounds* was recorded in two phases. First, he laid down the instrumental backing tracks at Gold Star, Western, and Sunset Sound. Then, when the traveling members of the Beach Boys were back in town, he overdubbed the vocals at Western and Columbia.

A good producer chooses the recording studio that best suits the feel of the music, and Brian chose his as carefully as he did a lyricist or musician. It was a detail that rang true in the quality of his productions—especially in that of *Pet Sounds*. "In the 1960s, each engineer and studio had their own individual sound," explains Bruce Botnick, who recorded "Here Today" at Sunset Sound. "There weren't console manufacturers, so each studio had its own unique console—and its own identity. You could always tell an Atlantic record from a Columbia record, or a Capitol record from an RCA record, by the sound of the consoles and microphones they used, the sound of their rooms, and their echo. Brian came to a studio for what the engineer and studio were doing."

Even the Beatles did not enjoy the luxury of recording outside of EMI's Abbey Road Studios, and the move signaled an important point in Brian's emergence as a producer. "Brian was saying, 'Look at what you can do with this recording studio,'" said Jimmy Webb. "Make no mistake: The recording studio was an instrument—Brian *made* it an instrument—and everybody was awed by what he was doing."

"Brian was always experimenting, trying something different, which made him unique," says Al Jardine. "Capitol was very structured. We couldn't touch the console in some of the studios, like at Columbia, which drove us all crazy! We all wanted to push up a control to increase our voice, or something. But they'd keep us away from the board, which was a problem for us. My gut feeling is that Brian just wanted the freedom to go where he wanted to go—and he wanted to work where Phil Spector worked."

Gold Star Recording Studios

Spector's Mecca was Gold Star Recording Studios, the birth-place of his famous "Wall of Sound." Located at 6252 Santa Monica Boulevard in Hollywood, the studio was founded in 1950 by Dave Gold and Stan Ross, and it quickly became a favorite among Hollywood's independent producers, who were looking to bypass costly union studios. "In order to record in those days, you had to pay union fees, and most of the people couldn't afford or didn't want to pay it," explains Larry Levine. "So, the union was not welcomed into the studio—we'd keep them out whenever we could manage to."

The late 1950s found the music industry on the cusp of the rock 'n' roll era, and with it came the birth of many small record labels. Gold Star became a breeding ground for upstart musicians recording their first records. "When I arrived at Gold Star in 1952, it was just a demo studio," Levine recalls. "In those days, we had one tape recorder. Young artists came in to make demos, and as the business changed, those demos became good enough to stand on their own as 'hit' records. The first real record I made there—one that started out as a demo—was Eddie Cochran's 'Summertime Blues' [1958]."

The size of the studio belied the fat, dense sound that was responsible for Gold Star's fame. "It was 20 by 22 feet, but the ceiling was very low," says Levine. "When people from New York saw it, they'd say, 'You're kidding! *This* is where all of that great sound is coming from?' When you hear a record, you picture in your mind what kind of place it was recorded in, and nobody believed it was created in such a small room, because on record, it sounded so spacy."

The Mono Wall

The heralded "Wall of Sound" was a dense, blasting panorama of musical texture that all but assaulted the listener. "I did all of Phil's records, and if it wasn't for Gold Star he would never have had a 'Wall of Sound,'" says guitarist Jerry Cole. "The studio and Gold Star's echo chambers *was* the 'Wall of Sound.'"

The studio and the echo chambers certainly had a lot to do with it, but as Levine explains, "A big part of it was the blending of instruments. Up to that point, most records featured a basic rhythm section. When Phil came along, we were suddenly using three pianos, three basses, and five or six guitars. That made all the difference in the world."

Spector's trademark sound was textured and thick. It was raw, thundering, and—most important—recorded in mono. "Phil always recorded in mono, because he felt that you could never come back to the exact mix again in stereo," Levine explains. "He'd say, 'I don't care how careful you are, the only way you can capture it—and keep it the way you have it—is in mono.'" Like his idol, Brian insisted on mixing his Beach Boys records, including *Pet Sounds*, in mono. "I think mono was great from the standpoint that there was no second guessing," said Chuck Britz. "You do certain things when you're mixing in mono: you equalize and use echo. Those are the things you do to make the sound big."

There was another reason why Spector and Wilson favored mono: it was the only format used for singles in the 1950s and '60s. Knowing that their tunes would likely be heard on car radios and cheaper home systems, they minimized the chance that their artfully crafted balances would be altered by the careless placement of stereo speakers by mixing directly to mono. Brian was so preoccupied with this that he sometimes auditioned his mixes through a car speaker set up in the control room in the Western studio.

Up until *Summer Days (and Summer Nights!!)* was recorded in 1965, Brian taped almost everything in mono, unless there was an overdub for additional instruments. "Half of *Summer Days . . .* was cut with the instruments spread out onto three tracks, which Brian mixed to mono on either another three- or four-track machine, or to the eight-track recorder at the CBS Studio," explains Mark Linett, a Grammy-nominated engineer and producer who now handles the remastering of the entire Beach Boys catalog at his recording studio in Glendale, California. "But remember—Brian never planned to use the multi-tracks to create a stereo record, and he never *monitored* in anything but mono."

In a conventional situation the multiple tracks would normally be mixed to two-track stereo for the final album master, but since he wasn't mixing the album in stereo, Brian reduced, or "bounced," the multiple instrumental tracks to a single monophonic track on another four-track tape, saving the three open tracks for vocal overdubs and instrumental sweetening. Later, the single instrumental track and the additional instrumental and vocal tracks were combined to create the album's mono master tape.

"In some instances, like on 'Sloop John B,' the second three-track tape was combined again to a third tape—in this case using a four-track machine—so that additional parts could be added," Linett says. "It was also not unusual for vocals or other instruments to be added 'live-to-tape,' as the mono mix was being made. Earlier Beach Boys songs that contain such overdubs are 'Help Me, Rhonda' and 'The Little Girl I Once Knew.' On *Pet Sounds*, both 'You Still Believe in Me' and 'Caroline No' had the lead vocal doubled live-to-tape as Chuck Britz was mixing the mono master."

Even though the end result was mono, Brian extracted the most from the multitrack technology of the day by recording on separate channels. This allowed him to layer the instrumental and vocal components that he'd recorded independently, giving him greater flexibility and control over the sound of his final mix.

Although the technology was simple, the creation of a well-balanced mono mix from multiple tracks required forethought and skill. "The limitations of recording three and four-track meant that you had to plan your strategy up front," explains engineer Joe Sidore, formerly of Western Recorders. "You had to know what you wanted to wind up with, and record things accordingly. You had to make your mix decisions on the spot, because combinations of instruments were often mixed together on the same track.

"You really had to know what the hell you were doing if you were mixing at that time, because you had to build your mixes from the very beginning. Brian and Chuck [Britz] were right on top of it. Brian didn't use tracks to just use them; there was a purpose behind everything he did. The multiple tracks were used intelligently."

As Bob Irwin explains, building a finely layered mono mix involves sensitivity and skill. "Creating a good mono mix is a conscious thing, especially when material is being sel-synced from one four-track machine to another. Someone is making careful decisions like, 'Where does that guitar live in the mix? If we're going to group everything on one track, where does this guitar go?'" Phil Ramone agrees. "There are placements for every instrument in the mono mix—they're great studies of contrast, texture, balance, and rhythm. For example, on 'Here Today,' the combination of wet and dry sounds on the vocals and the distinctive sound of the organ and baritone sax give it incredible dimension.

"Pet Sounds is the ultimate album to use in illustrating the beauty of a mono mix and the way that things can be understated, yet play such an important part that your mind automatically lifts them up and out of the mix. That's the secret of a good mix, and if you're in the business of making records you'd best understand it. Brian certainly did," adds Irwin.

As Irwin points out, the beauty of a well-executed mono mix like Pet Sounds is the feel of the recording. Certain sounds seem to hover just above the threshold of hearing, as if they're perceived but not heard. The rise and fall of the French horn at the end of "God Only Knows" illustrates this: it's discernible on the stereo mix, but remains a mere whisper on the mono. Yet, even if you'd never heard the stereo mix, you'd swear that the French horn had been prominent in that passage all along. Ditto the honky-tonk sounding tack

Brian Wilson directs a session from the booth, Gold Star Studios, circa 1966.

Left *Beach Boys publicity shot, circa 1962: (clockwise from top left) Mike Love, Brian Wilson, Carl Wilson, Dennis Wilson, and Al Jardine.*

Above *Audree and Murry Wilson, circa early 1960s.*

Left *Enigmatic record producer Phil Spector at the Gold Star Studio mixing console, Hollywood.*

Right *The Four Freshmen: (clockwise from front) Ross Barbour, Don Barbour, Bob Flanigan, and Ken Albers, circa 1956.*

Above left *Magic moment: Brian thoughtfully studies a playback.*

Above right *Gifted copywriter-turned-lyricist Tony Asher, circa 1966.*

Above *(left to right) Bruce Johnston, Carl Wilson, Al Jardine, Dennis Wilson, and Mike Love.*

Above *At the mikes: Vocal overdub session at Western Studio 3: Carl Wilson (left) and Bruce Johnston (right).*

Searching for perfection, Brian rehearses "the boys" during a vocal session, Western Studio 3.

Above left *Locking in the tempo: Brian's reliable timekeeper Hal Blaine on drums.*

Above right *In the control room at Western Studio 3: Recording engineer Chuck Britz (seated), Brian Wilson, and second engineer Winston Wong.*

Above *Incomparable Fender bassist Carol Kaye (left), recording with jazz guitarist Tommy Tedesco at Gold Star.*

The band frolics during the Pet Sounds *cover shoot at the San Diego Zoo: (left to right) Al Jardine, Mike Love, Dennis Wilson, Brian Wilson, and Carl Wilson.*

Latter-day genius: Brian Wilson, London, January 27, 2002.

piano buried deep within the "sometimes I feel very sad" theme on "I Just Wasn't Made for These Times."

Don Was (who produced the 1995 film and CD *I Just Wasn't Made for These Times*) discussed the aura created by a good mono mix with Rick Rosen in the June 1997 issue of *Stereophile*. "Leaving some of the stuff to the imagination—creating textures by blending and viewing the whole as opposed to isolating the components—is good." Not everyone agreed. As musician-producer Steve Douglas correctly observed, "A lot of times, some beautiful, orchestrated stuff got lost in his mixes."

While they shared a love for mono sound, Phil Spector and Brian Wilson maintained different philosophies when it came to production. While Spector went for the sound, Wilson aimed for the performance. "Phil Spector knew how to create hit sounds—there's no getting around that," says Jerry Cole. "But Brian Wilson was far superior intellectually and musically, and he hit the mark far more often than Spector. Brian and Phil were a world apart."

Violinist Sid Sharp concurs. "Phil was an incredible producer, but Brian was *music*, and that's the difference. Brian's music emanated from him—it just came out of him. Phil was technical, and he knew exactly what people wanted. Brian was naive and shy, but when it came to his music, he knew exactly what he wanted to do."

Chuck Britz and Western Studio 3
When it came to recording, the person who truly understood Brian was Chuck Britz, who became his "personal engineer" and, in a greater sense, his coproducer. "Chuck was a

surrogate father for Brian," believes Murray McFadden, Britz's second engineer during the early 1970s. "He was also friendly with Murry Wilson, so he sometimes served as a liaison in the acrimonious relationship between Brian and his dad."

Britz, who died in August 2000, began his career at the Los Angeles studios of C. P. MacGregor, recording big bands for the U.S. Government's Armed Forces Radio Service. Later, he took a position at Western. By the time Brian Wilson arrived to make Beach Boys records there in 1963, Britz had engineered dozens of rock 'n' roll hits in Western Studio 3.

Britz once explained how he convinced Wilson to record more of the group's backing tracks in his studio. "Brian said he wanted the 'Wall of Sound,'" he explained. "He was recording the instrumentals at Gold Star, and I was doing the vocal sessions for him at Western. One day I said, 'Brian, how come you give me all the hard work? I get you guys balanced and sounding great, and then I mix it down for you . . . ' He said, 'This studio is too small.' I said, 'Give me a chance. It'll be tight, but I guarantee that we can do it.' The session after that, he let me do the band, and after that, we recorded the band at Western almost all the time."

Located at 6000 Sunset Boulevard, Western Studio 3 was part of Bill Putnam's United Recording Corporation. By the time he opened the Western facility, Putnam was already a legend in the recording business. "Bill Putnam was the father of recording as we know it today," explains engineer Bruce Swedien. "The processes and designs we take for granted— the design of modern recording desks, the way components are laid out and the way they function, console design, cue sends, echo returns, and multitrack switching—all originated in Bill's imagination."

"Western 3 wasn't a huge room, but it was big enough to fit a rhythm section and percussion and horns at the same time," says Joe Sidore. "It was small but comfortable, and had a good sound. The rooms at Western had their own identity, and were perfect to record in. When you walked out of any one of those rooms, whatever you had on tape just sounded like a record. It had a certain polished quality. It was a record! The echo—developed by Hal Halverson—was one of our signatures."

Sidore remembers that Wilson appreciated the privacy Western afforded him. "When the Beach Boys were working at Western, there would always be lines of musicians out in the hall, drinking coffee while Brian worked in the studio with the other musicians. Studio 3 was also one of the more intimate and private rooms in the complex; you weren't going to have people traipsing through the hall while you were recording. That's one of the reasons Brian liked it so much, although Chuck had a lot to do with it too."

In Britz, Brian found the ultimate champion: a faithful friend and colleague who never stopped believing in the veracity of his music. "Before he died, Chuck told me that he felt the music was going to live a long time, and that he'd always felt like Brian was really on to something very great," says bassist Carol Kaye. "He loved Brian. He truly loved him."

Britz was flexible, but he was also firm enough to deal with Brian's eccentricities. "Brian could get anyone mad," Britz once said. "He was trying to get out of his head in musical terms what he wants to hear. A lot of the guys would laugh, because they couldn't hear the parts [as he was hearing them]." As Joe Sidore explains, "With Chuck, all an artist had to do was think about what they were bringing to the session. Other than communicating a concept to him, you could leave him alone and focus on your own stuff, because you knew that he was doing his part. He got a lot of input from Brian, and then became Brian's interpreter. Brian could tell him what he wanted, and Chuck knew how to get it."

Britz's experience recording all types of music was a huge asset. "Chuck was a practical engineer," says Murray McFadden. "His philosophy was, 'Start on time, get the job done, and go home.' He wasn't meticulous—I've worked with the anal retentive, insane 'attention to detail' types, and he was the antithesis of that." According to Sidore, few of Western's engineers could match Britz's fine technical sense. "He knew how to use the equipment that was available to him, and extracted the most sound out of everything that he recorded so it sounded tight and natural. His choice of microphones, his microphone placement and equalizing technique, and the careful use of limiters pulled everything together. And the way he mixed made a big difference, too."

Long before the client lounge became a studio's calling card, Chuck Britz had learned the importance of a relaxed atmosphere. When the pressure mounted, Brian would sometimes leave the studio for a break, playing pinball on a machine that had been specially rigged by the engineer. "There was a pinball machine in the hallway," remembers Dean Britz, who was a teenager at the time. "My dad had it fixed so that you didn't need quarters to play. There was a slug on a string, and that's where I would hang out on the rare occasion that I visited the studio."

More often than not, Chuck was the group's "safety valve," tempering Brian's intensity with a measure of well-placed levity. "Chuck maintained a very cool disposition, but he was working under extreme pressure," Brian once explained. "He was working with five guys who were out of their minds—and he kept his cool. Chuck was always saying, 'I've got to get out of here by 6:30, because I have a bowling tournament.' And we'd say, 'C'mon, let's get to work. We're gonna lose Chuck!'"

CBS and Sunset Sound

While Western and Gold Star remained Brian's favored studios, he recorded portions of *Pet Sounds* in other places. For a time, the Columbia Records studio located in the CBS complex at Sunset and Gower became a favorite place to tape the group's vocal sessions. The studio was home to Columbia Records artists including the Byrds and Paul Revere and the Raiders. Brian was enthusiastic about recording there, as they had one of the first eight-track tape machines in town.

"I was working with Terry Melcher on our 'Bruce & Terry' records," says Bruce Johnston. "One day we were at the CBS studio, and Terry went into a closet, where he found an eight-track machine that the Columbia engineers had cobbled together from some spare Ampex parts. He asked them what the machine was for. 'Oh, you don't want to use that—it's not working well,' they told him. Terry persisted. 'We use it for Duke Ellington and Percy Faith, so we can have separation of instruments,' they explained. Terry started using it for our sessions. More often than not, the motor would malfunction and the tape would come spooling off the reel, crinkled and damaged. We'd have to call the session."

Spoiled by the luxury of recording on eight tracks, Brian began recording his instrumental tracks at either Gold Star or Western, bouncing them to a single mono track on the eight-track tape machine at Columbia, and using the seven remaining tracks for vocal overdubs and sweetening. For *Pet Sounds*, the eight track machine was used to record vocals for five songs: "God Only Knows," "Here Today," "Wouldn't It Be Nice," "I'm Waiting for the Day," and "I Just Wasn't Made for These Times."

The instrumental backing for "Here Today" was recorded at Sunset Sound (5200 Sunset Boulevard), two miles west of United/Western Recording. Walt Disney Records music director Tutti Camarata built the studio, which once housed an automotive repair garage. In the early 1960s, it was the only non-film studio in Los Angeles to boast a self-contained isolation booth.

Brian tried the studio at the suggestion of saxophonist Steve Douglas, who admired the work of Sunset engineer Bruce Botnick. "As a producer, Brian wanted the sound I was getting at Sunset, and that's why he came back after *Pet Sounds* to do other things," explains Botnick. "It was a bright, punchy room with brick walls and an asphalt-tiled floor, but pretty sounding just the same. I used nothing but tube microphones, primarily Sony C-37As and Neumann U47s. Our echo chamber was unique, as was the way I'd treat the echo.

"Brian was meticulous—constantly making changes from take to take. I found him to be terrifically creative, and very egoless about it. He didn't come in and try to take over. Some producers I've worked with would come in and look at all the microphones and approve the microphones we were using, and where things were placed. Brian never did any of that. He knew what he wanted, but was totally open to a different interpretation if it came along. The music always came first, the sound second. Since we didn't have many tracks available to us, the feel of the band was everything."

The Wrecking Crew

By the early 1960s, the West Coast music scene was teeming with first-rate players working in Hollywood's film, television, and recording studios. Many had classical training, while others specialized in backing country, pop, rock, or jazz performers. It was from this pool that Phil Spector (and, consequently, Brian Wilson) handpicked the session band from a group of studio musicians that later came to be known as "the Wrecking Crew."

"None of us ever called ourselves 'the Wrecking Crew' back in the '60s—that was totally unheard of," explains Carol Kaye. "Some musicians don't like the term; we were all independent, freelance professionals, and were totally interchangeable in all the studio work we did. There were never just one or two rhythm sections, or one specific group that got called on all the time. Everyone worked with everyone else. When we walked in the door, they knew it was going to be a hit record."

The term "Wrecking Crew" was first used in the 1920s to describe the fiercely loyal employees of San Francisco Chronicle publisher William Randolph Hearst. During the

1980s, it was the name of singer Darlene Love's backup group. In 1990, Hal Blaine adopted the slogan to describe Spector's core team of players. "It came about because that was the impression we gave the older musicians," Blaine says. "The established musicians wore blue blazers and neckties, and always cleaned their ashtrays after a date. We were the new guys, and we dressed as we lived: in Levis and T-shirts. We were informal and spontaneous, and a lot of the old hands thought we were wrecking the music industry."

Their reputation became so great that many bands, including the Byrds, Paul Revere and the Raiders, and Simon and Garfunkel, used the studio players to fill out their ranks. "They were as ubiquitous as Clearasil commercials in the '60s," says Mark Lindsay of the Raiders. "This is not to say that group members did not play on their own records. It was just that the pressure of making another charttopper sometimes caused producers to take shortcuts. 'The band's out on the road? No sweat—call the Crew!'"

As Brian's music changed, he began tapping the Crew to record instrumental tracks while the Beach Boys were out on tour. "Brian was evolving very fast," remembered Carl Wilson. "He was writing stuff that really needed to be performed—that's why he needed session players."

To music aficionados, the names of Brian's favored instrumentalists are familiar. The stalwarts included Hal Blaine (drums), Glen Campbell and Billy Strange (guitar), Al de Lory (piano), Steve Douglas (sax), Carol Kaye (Fender bass), Larry Knechtel (Hammond B3 organ), Don Randi (piano), Lyle Ritz (acoustic bass), and Julius Wechter (percussion). Ray Pohlman often doubled on Fender bass and guitar. In addition to the regulars, several well known jazz and pop musicians often joined in, including Frank Capp (percussion), Plas Johnson and Jay Migliori (sax), Barney Kessel, Bill Pitman, Howard Roberts, and Tommy Tedesco (guitar), and Lew McCreary (trombone). For added color, Brian called on specialists like Roy Caton (trumpet), Carl Fortina and Frank Marocco (accordion), Tommy Morgan (bass harmonica), Alan Robinson (French horn), and Paul Tanner (Electro-Theremin). Sid Sharp arranged the strings, which provided an appropriate measure of tenderness.

For the players in highest demand, the lifestyle of a Hollywood studio musician was grueling. "My day started at 8:00 A.M. at Universal Studios," explains guitarist Bill Pitman. "Five days later, I was still doing the same thing, and getting home at four o'clock in the morning. By the end of the day, I felt nothing but exhaustion."

The pace was fast, the burnout rate high. "The rollover was tremendous," says Larry Knechtel, who played keyboards on *Pet Sounds*, and later, the famous piano solo on Simon and Garfunkel's "Bridge Over Troubled Water." "If you got five years in, you were doing well. The producers would change, or they'd want to hear something fresh. I didn't experience that—I was very lucky. At one point, I didn't take a vacation for three years, 'cause I was afraid that if I went away, the phone wouldn't ring anymore."

The musicians were energized by the moments that tested their mettle. "Studio work is 99 percent boredom, and 1 percent sheer panic,'" says Pitman. "There was really nothing to play that stretched us 99 percent of the time, but that 1 percent was enough to make up for everything else. All of a sudden there comes a point where you were really stretched to the limits of your ability—to the point that you thought that maybe you wouldn't be able to do it. That tension is what kept it interesting musically."

From the moment he began using the Wrecking Crew, Brian's music acquired new depth and dimension. "The whole band was fantastic—I'd say we had the top band in Los Angeles," said Chuck Britz. "There wasn't a guy in town who could outplay anyone on our sessions. Even the 'seconds' I occasionally had to take on the first half hour of a session were better than 90 percent of the rest of the guys in town."

Brian appreciated jazz, and the improvisational skills of those players versed in the idiom. "The essence of jazz music is improvisation," says Hal Lifson. "There wasn't much room in rock music for improvisation, but because the musicians worked for hours on end during the *Pet Sounds* sessions, they would improvise riffs that became part of the recording."

Jazz strains abound in Wilson's melodies—and not just because the players were interpreting them that way. It was a *feel* that emanated from within. "It didn't matter what Brian was recording—when he sat down at the piano, he was a jazz player," says guitarist Billy Strange. "I think he created a jazz feel that worked with his rock 'n' roll and surf music—it was the perfect marriage. That's the way it felt. Brian would never say, 'I want an open G chord here'—it was never that simple. He'd ask for a G6 plus 9 kind of chord. He'd always find some weird combination to make it work, and the feel always had a jazz configuration."

Tony Asher recalls introducing Brian to a number of jazz standards during the *Pet Sounds* writing process. "Brian and I talked a lot about music. He didn't know much about jazz or jazz standards, but he knew the Four Freshmen. So I said, 'The Four Freshmen are a jazz vocal group, and there are all kinds of wonderful jazz songs with harmonies and chord changes that I think would really interest you.' Brian looked at me inquisitively. I had piqued his interest! 'Oh yeah, like what?' he asked. I played him 'Stella by Starlight,' which is one of my favorites. Not that I think it's the greatest song ever written—but it does have some nice chord changes. I remembered that 'The Warmth of the Sun' makes a key change by the second bar, so I knew he'd dig hearing some of the standards that made similar changes.

"After that, Brian pulled out some of his own jazz albums, and I brought over some of my own. I played him a number of tunes that I thought he'd like: Ellington's 'Sophisticated Lady' was one, and Hampton Hawes's version of 'All the Things You Are,' which not only makes key changes, but also goes through the entire circle of fifths. I thought that would impress him. He was always 100 percent absorbed in listening, and I could tell he was blown away by some of the things I played for him."

The Arranger

The session players' ease with improvisation proved invaluable when it came to recording, because unlike schooled arrangers who wrote out each part, Brian communicated his *Pet Sounds* charts to the musicians in an unusual way: he hummed or sang it to them at the recording session. There were no pre-session rehearsals, and Brian would rarely arrive at the studio with more than a sketchy musical draft in hand.

"We used to work with 'chord charts,'" recalls Hal Blaine. "He wouldn't write on score paper—he'd write the chords he felt on a piece of regular paper, and then photocopy it when he got to the studio. Everyone would get the same copy; we'd listen to the song, make some notes, and then go with it. If Brian wanted something different than what we played, we'd mark it on the chart."

Of all his musicians, Brian relied most on Blaine, who set the tempo for the band. "Brian used to call me into the booth to listen to playbacks, because he wanted to know whether or not the tempo was perfect." The most prolific studio musician in the business, Blaine was known for his dependability and superior technique. "My sound on Brian's dates was basically the Phil Spector sound, with a few minor adjustments," he says. "Phil liked a high, tight snare sound because he wanted it to cut through the 'Wall.' I always played the snare and floor tom in unison to strengthen the backbeat. For Brian, I modified the snare to a lower sound, and combined it with the floor tom." Blaine also helped flesh out Brian's bare-bones arrangements.

Brian's vague sketches were very different than the carefully prepared arrangements that his musicians were used to sight-reading. "It was evident that he wrote the music, and that he was not trained in writing it well—which made his efforts even more remarkable," explains Carol Kaye. "The notes were sometimes on the wrong sides of the stems. Sharps and flats were incorrectly noted. But it was *his* music—he knew it well, and, unlike making up our own parts like we did for the other groups we recorded with, we played what Brian wanted."

The manner in which Brian wrote—the chords, the keys and the key changes that he used, and the rhythmic devices that he incorporated into his compositions—have as much to do with the emotional effect of his music as does the lyric or the choice of instrumentation. "Brian's chords were wonderful," says pianist Don Randi. "I liken him to the Bill Evans of rock 'n' roll. He could hear things that a lot of other people couldn't, and would attempt things that they'd *never* try."

Although he wasn't writing according to strict standards, Brian adapted many compositional techniques found in more involved music. "Since he wasn't a classical pianist, he didn't think classically; he thought within the framework in which he was comfortable," says bass harmonica player Tommy Morgan. "Brian would write the chords and the sounds on each beat: he assigned very specific chords and sounds to every beat of each measure. He didn't write horizontally, as in classical composition; he wrote vertically, in block chords. In doing so, he would play the chord on the right hand, and put another chord against it—a chord where some of the notes don't fit. That lends it polytonality, or more than one tonality, and the effect is incredible."

Unusual keys also helped to punch up a melody's emotional content. "He wasn't afraid of offbeat keys—he had an affinity for the keys that musicians tend to avoid," explains vocal arranger David Wright. "'You Still Believe in Me' is in the key of B, which is unusual (keyboard players tend to avoid it, as it's a half step away from C, which has no sharps or flats.) For 'That's Not Me,' he chose the key of F sharp— the most distant key a composer could write in."

Throughout *Pet Sounds* we can hear subtle harmonic modulations—key changes—that heighten the music's strength and suggest upward or downward motion. The practice of modulating major or minor thirds in a pop song was born of Tin Pan Alley songwriters such as Irving Berlin, who would often start a song in one key, shift to another mid-song, and then end up back in the original key for the conclusion. In building the arrangements for *Pet Sounds*, Brian used the technique liberally.

"There are tertian shifts all over 'Wouldn't It Be Nice,'" Wright explains. "The intro of the song is in A, but the song itself turns out to be in the key of F—down a major third. Then, the bridge is in D. There are a lot of thirds in that harmonic motion, and Brian definitely liked to move away a third, and then work his way back to the original key. On 'That's Not Me,' he begins in F sharp, progresses to A (a minor third upward), then moves back to F sharp. It's an old harmonic game, but one that you don't often find in pop music. Brian came up with melodies that lead you around and into a lot of different chords and harmonies before the song ends. Whatever he came up with—instrumentally or vocally—always involved a vast array of harmony."

Rhythmically, Brian's work is punctuated by irregular breaks in tempo that heighten its dramatic effect. On *Pet Sounds*, both "Wouldn't It Be Nice" and "You Still Believe in Me" change tempo throughout the song. "Bringing the tempo to a stopping point and then resuming it is a risky thing in pop music," says Wright. "Usually, the idea is to keep the rhythm moving along steadily, so people can dance to it. It was unusual for pop composers to experiment so widely with tempo. Changing the tempo—or stopping it altogether—implies that you expect people are listening to the song."

On the Date: The Tracking Sessions

Brian stored the ideas for his unusual musical gestures in his head until the day of recording. And, since he arranged and rehearsed the songs in sections, the musicians rarely heard an entire tune until they began to record it. "Brian's dates were completely disorganized," says accordionist Frank Marocco. "When you first walked in, it was like chaos—you never knew what was going to happen. You'd be thinking, 'Geez, how is this going to end up sounding like something?' But by the end of the session it would come together and sound like what Brian had in mind all along. I sometimes think he put it together as he went along."

The unstructured studio atmosphere was deceiving—a mask for Brian's restlessness. "As disorganized as he could otherwise be, when Brian was in the studio you got the impression that if he didn't get his ideas down on tape as quickly as possible, they'd slip away from him," says Tony Asher. "He wanted to keep things moving, and he drove the guys a little. He created just the right amount of tension to get what he wanted done." Despite outward appearances, however, there was always a plan. Before the session, Brian would sit for hours, working out keys and chord structures at the piano. And while he generally stuck to this mental blueprint, he always welcomed suggestions from the band.

"Brian had a broad scope of musical knowledge," says percussionist Frank Capp. "Sometimes he knew what he wanted to hear, but not how to achieve the sound. He might say, 'I want something shimmery,' or 'I want it to sound like something blowing in the wind.' I'd suggest a percussive effect to suit the image he had in mind. I had a plethora of percussion instruments and gimmicks at that time, so I could usually find something that would work. I'd play him two or three things, and he would choose what he liked best. On other occasions, he knew exactly what he wanted, and would call for that. It was a cooperative thing; we contributed our ability and talent to what he had in mind."

Although it was unusual, there was something to be said for writing and rehearsing the arrangements on the spot. In a way, it added an immediacy that could easily be lost with a preconceived, formulaic orchestration. "He would come in with an idea, but as the hours went by, he was discovering things he hadn't thought of," percussionist Julius Wechter told David Leaf. "When he heard something he liked, his eyes would light up and he would say, 'Don't change that; it's perfect. Write it down.'"

As Tommy Morgan explained, the musicians felt this gentle give-and-take worked to everyone's advantage. "If it wasn't working, Brian would say, 'OK, how about this?' He could size up a musical situation in an instant, because he knew what he was trying to create. If he had something in mind that was impossible to create, he would change it."

Though Brian afforded them wide latitude, the musicians respected the integrity of his vision and didn't overstep their boundaries. "We were accompaniment—the vocals were the main part of the records," says Don Randi. "What we provided was coloring—*orchestration*. If you do too much, you're in the way. You had to know that you couldn't go crazy."

Jerry Cole's irresistible guitar intro to "Wouldn't It Be Nice" illustrates how this sympathetic collaboration affected the music: the passage's quirky effervescence announces the cheerful tone of the song while setting the stage for the album's complexity. "Brian came up with the opening—that was his baby," Cole explains. "It was just a texture, a metallic kind of sound that he heard and liked."

As Mark Linett explains, the recording of the guitar intro created an unusual situation in the recording studio. "Jerry's 12-string was played directly into the console at Gold Star. Only those in the control room—and Hal Blaine, who was wearing headphones—could hear him play. Hal needed to hear the 12-string intro since he was responsible for listening carefully and bringing the rest of the band in on cue. Running the guitar direct into the console was something Brian did because it provided a different sort of sound to the instrument, especially when reverb was added and it was combined with the other instruments. (The reverb was added 'live,' and printed directly to tape.) A 12-string in particular sounds good when "di'd" (direct injected) into the console, and is still often recorded that way today. It's also important to note that in 1966, the electric basses were recorded with a microphone and a bass amp. Beginning around 1969, though, most engineers began 'double' recording the basses—they would mike the amp and record it, and also record it 'direct,' to give it more clarity and isolation. It is a practice that continues to this day."

Another texture that adds to the happy feel of "Wouldn't It Be Nice" is the expansive sound of twin accordions, which in this case play a melody bearing a striking resemblance to the unique organ phrases on the introduction of the band's 1965 classic "California Girls." To achieve this, Brian engaged two of Hollywood's top accordionists, Carl Fortina and Frank Marocco. As the recording evolved, Brian took particular care to keep the instrument in the foreground:

About one minute into Take 9:
"Hold it! We lost the accordion sound. Where'd it go? You're both up in the same register, I hope. Let me hear you guys alone . . . . "

Then, during the introduction on Take 12:
"Accordions, stay in that same, groovy thing we had because if we lose it . . . it's that certain vibration or frequency thing. When you're both about the same distance it comes through great."

"We were playing the same thing, but using a different configuration of reeds on our instruments," says Marocco. "The accordion is a multi-reed instrument. There are nine sets of reeds that could be compared to harmonicas of different sizes. You can use any configuration of reeds: if you want a tiny, delicate sound like a concertina, you use the single piccolo reed—the smallest in the accordion. If you want a big, full, brassy sound, you engage all of the reeds. There are different degrees and combinations of reeds you can use: bassoon, clarinet, flute, oboe, and violin reeds. The accordion was the first synthesizer; it could produce different sounds by the engagement of the reeds."

The way Brian melded the accordions into "Wouldn't It Be Nice" is so skillful that in the bridge ("You know it seems the more we talk about it . . . ") they sound like a complement of violins playing a sustained tremolo. Marocco devised the texture for this song. "To make that sound, Carl and I played the same part in unison to achieve a chorusing effect. We probably used the violin reeds to get the string sound. I remember that session well, because I played a triple bellow shake, quickly moving the bellows in and out to simulate a shaking sound [the imaginary violins in the bridge!] Brian really liked that, but I created a real monster, because I had to do that for the whole session, one take after another. I was as sore as hell, and remember going home saying, 'Never again will I tell anyone I can do that!'"

Marocco's exasperation is appreciable, and it underscores the resolve with which Brian worked. He wouldn't hesitate to put a musician through his or her paces if the effort helped achieve the precise shading he desired. While the tracking sessions could be long and tedious, they were—according to most of the musicians—"productive and fun." Brian thrived on the collegial relationship he enjoyed with his musicians, and he treated them with respect. As he worked on perfecting a recording, he'd balance firm decisiveness with gentle encouragement. "I think we can have a better sound there," he might say, or "C'mon, let's get back to that nice, groovy feel we had before." Every musician who worked closely with him agrees that Brian approached the process of recording with "enthusiastic professionalism."

To a person, the players who worked with him appreciated Brian's making them feel like equal partners in the recording process. "He really respected musicians," said Julius Wechter. "There were [some] leaders (like Spector) who just treated musicians like paid employees—like machines. Brian used to come out of the booth, shake hands with everyone. It was more like a party. We got the feeling we were helping create the sound; after the session, we felt like we had left some creative juice there. I think one of the reasons for Brian's success at those sessions was that he stuck with the same guys. He didn't have to come out each time and introduce himself to a bunch of strangers; we just went in and started playing the tune."

Although he nurtured a warm, professional atmosphere, his keen wit set the tone when recording. "Brian was droll—very dry," says Carol Kaye. "His humor was subtle. He would get that 'studio stare' look. In the early studio days, you didn't crack a smile or arch an eyebrow. You'd sit there, still as a statue, and Brian adopted that look. You didn't know whether he was kidding or not. Brian knew more than anyone that in the studio, time is money—you didn't go there to have fun. There's a certain amount of fun that you will have, but you get your laugh in, and then you get back to business."

Brian wove a wealth of humor into his melodies, a quality that stems from his dry wit and a love for Walt Disney. "He had a total infatuation with Disney—mainly *Mary Poppins* and films of that era," says Hal Lifson. "The look and sound of the Disney films was important in bringing a symphonic element to Brian's music; animated sounds like bass harmonica were those that might be heard in a cartoon. Hal Blaine playing the water bottle on 'Caroline No' is brilliant—it's a sound effect that you'd expect to hear in a Disney movie." (Originally, the song began with an instrumental introduction, but as the session progressed, Brian decided to have

Blaine strike the bottom of a plastic Sparkletts water cooler jug with a hard percussion mallet to punctuate the opening.)

The introduction to "Wouldn't It Be Nice" is another prime example of Brian's predilection for whimsy. Jerry Cole's detuned guitar helps conjure up the sound of a calliope, giving us the impression that the characters are at a carnival, riding the merry-go-round. Likewise, the imaginative use of bicycle bell, bicycle horn, and finger cymbals on "You Still Believe in Me" helps evoke a juvenile air that mirrors the immature attitude projected by the lyric.

These accents add meaning, color, and zest. "Music represents color, and people forget that," explains Cole. "Some music is red, some is yellow, some is orange, some is blue, and some is black. Brian was able to color his music well, as far as making the sound fit the mode and the song." The sterling brilliance of "Sloop John B" exemplifies this: the arrangement is a refreshing blend of rock and marching band instrumentation in which flutes, glockenspiel, and baritone sax meet bass, guitar, and drums, creating a celebratory tone that contributes significantly to the song's melodiousness.

Brian took extra pains to infuse his charts with unusual sounds and unexpected instrumental pairings, and a plethora of color came from his use of novel instruments. Thus, exotic percussion, guiros, steel guitars, vibes, bass flutes, and harmonicas were juxtaposed against traditional instruments in Brian Wilson's pop orchestra. "The music had grace and spirit, so much so that it could be orchestrated across a wide spectrum of musical styles," said Nik Venet. "Brian composed and produced musical effects like the first viewing of a sunrise to a once-blind person."

The eerie, sitar-style introduction to "You Still Believe in Me" is a case in point. Brian and lyricist Tony Asher experimented for hours to create the ghostly texture, which was recorded 11 weeks after the original tracking session. "We were aiming for the sound of a harpsichord, but we really wanted something more ethereal," Asher explains. "Brian held down the keys on the keyboard, and I leaned way inside the piano to pluck the strings so they'd ring. If you pluck the open strings, they sound pretty good. We worked for quite a while, and I tried everything: hairpins, bobby pins, paper clips, and my fingers. We did take after take, but we finally got the sound that Brian wanted."

On the album's ninth track, "I Know There's an Answer," Brian used the funkiness of Tommy Morgan's bass harmonica to lend the tune an ominous, foreboding sound. "Brian used instruments imaginatively," Morgan said. "Not many people used bass harmonica at that time—Brian certainly used it before the Beatles. My solo on 'I Know There's an Answer' was improvised, but whenever I played as part of the bass line, I played exactly what Brian told me to play." On the session:

Morgan: *Brian, do you want me to lay out again after that instrumental break, and then come back in with the fours toward the end?*

Brian: *We're gonna have you wail on that baby for the instrumental break. Think you can do it?*

Morgan: *I'll play it straight through this time.*

Brian: *Try to wail. Do a thing—you know.*

The strangest thing that Brian used was the Electro-Theremin, which he featured on "I Just Wasn't Made for These Times." His fascination with the instrument began when he was a child. "When I was an eight-year-old kid, my dad and mom took me over to their friend's house, and they had a Theremin," he explained. "The guy was playing it, and I was scared to death of that sound—it really frightened me a lot. I really got scared. I didn't want to hear that sound. It sounded like one of those horrible scary movies—weird trip, weird facial expressions—almost sexual."

The Theremin was an electronic instrument developed in 1919 by Russian inventor Leon Theremin. Its appeal was as much visual as audible: a Theremin player could create quite a show, moving his or her hands around the contraption's antennae to produce a surreal, space-aged sound. During the 1920s and '30s the device was mass-produced and marketed by RCA as an ideal home instrument. Interest in the Theremin's peculiar tone was rekindled in 1945, when film composer Miklos Rosza featured it in the score for Alfred Hitchcock's *Spellbound*.

UCLA music professor and trombonist Dr. Paul Tanner developed the Electro-Theremin with electronics wizard Bob Whitesell in 1958, and played it on *Pet Sounds* eight years later. Unlike a traditional Theremin, Tanner's instrument was played like a keyboard, and it had a slightly different sound. "The Electro-Theremin didn't have the fine tonal quality of a real Theremin, but our instrument was much easier to play and sounded so close that the people hiring me thought it was a Theremin," Tanner explains. "We didn't know what to call it, so we settled on the name 'Electro-Theremin.'

The prototype was finished just hours before the premiere recording session on which the instrument made its debut [a 1958 album called *Music for Heavenly Bodies*]."

Tanner—a big-band musician who played in the original Glenn Miller band—was aware of the Beach Boys and was surprised when Brian placed the call himself. "Brian phoned and spoke to my wife," Tanner recalls. "I was on a record date, but she knew that the person I was playing for had never heard of overtime! She told him that I would be through with that session at 11:00 P.M. Brian said, 'Good. Then my session will start at 11:30.' She called me, and I went to the studio when I finished the other session, and Brian started putting little pieces of the melody together."

To Tanner, the sessions were interminable. "We'd work all night long, and then get called back a couple of days later to put *more* pieces together. We never had any idea what we were doing." Brian admired the haunting quality of Tanner's contraption, and he would go on to use it on two later songs: "Good Vibrations" and "Wild Honey."

Brian employed unusual sounds well. As an example, he accentuated the eccentric sound of the Electro-Theremin on "I Just Wasn't Made for These Times" by including harpsichord, tack piano, flutes, temple blocks, timpani, banjo, and harmonica. The Fender bass also took a leading role: played melodically behind the voices, it becomes a focus of attention. But while he sometimes ventured outside conventional limits, Brian also stuck to the traditional, giving strings, woodwinds, and brass star billing alongside guitar, bass, and drums. "He had no qualms about mixing a classical instrument with a pop instrument," says Phil Ramone. "Oboe against electric guitar or tack piano, tambourine against strings. He used percussion—mallets and timpani—like a classical orchestrator or a composer writing for the ballet. It's as if he has no limitations, and his work as an arranger definitely opened the door for all of us."

With "Caroline No" Brian reached an instrumental pinnacle. The arrangement is so impressive it could easily stand on its own, sans vocals. In the intro, the interplay between bass and percussion is choreographed with ballet-like precision. (Listen for the rhythmic pattern created by the Fender bass, water jug, tambourine, muted bells, and shaker—a pattern that continues throughout the song.) The percussion—wind chimes in particular—plays a key role in extending the breezy feel of the performance.

On this song, the standard rhythm section is augmented with harpsichord, ukulele, and percussion. Vibes (with tremolo) and wind chimes add a whimsical touch. But it's the flutes and saxophones that really make the difference, infusing the melody with an enchanting glow. The flute and bass flute are doubled (they play the same melody but one octave apart), creating a thick, warm texture; the total effect of this shines through in the second chorus, when the flutes repeat the melody ("Where did your long hair go?"). The emotional stakes are raised considerably when the saxophone pipes in as Brian sings, " . . . break my heart/I want to go and cry." Throughout, the liberal use of major seventh chords affords the track a melancholy feeling.

For some songs, Brian wrote exceptional string parts, relying on Sid Sharp (who had played under Leopold Stokowski) to interpret them. "We often added the strings during 'sweetening' sessions, although we would sometimes play live with the band," Sharp said. "When we sweetened, Brian would say, 'I hear raindrops,' and I'd have the strings play pizzicato (which makes a plucking sound), or spiccato, with a jumping bow. Jesse Ehrlich—a cellist and composer with a remarkable ear—would help transcribe and notate the parts. Brian was sensitive and kind, and that emotion is reflected in the string parts he came up with."

Two songs illustrate Brian's deft integration of traditional instruments into a rock arrangement: "I'm Waiting for the Day" and "Don't Talk (Put Your Head on My Shoulder)."

On "I'm Waiting for the Day," he interjects an unexpected string interlude before the final chorus, emphasizing the lower register. In this seven-second passage we glimpse Brian's refined musical sense, and his predilection for taking us by surprise. Here, the theme is arbitrary—it isn't voiced anywhere else in the song. In this short section, the string ensemble sweeps through an interesting sequence of 10 chords, none of which repeat.

But the coalescence of instrumental and lyric lines on *Pet Sounds* reached a peak with "Don't Talk (Put Your Head on My Shoulder)," the beauty of which was appreciated by Tony Asher. "I always thought that this song was one hell of an example of Brian's musical sophistication," he explains. "He rarely used strings on his records, and I was astonished to learn that he could write for a string quartet. The arrangement he came up with for this song is so emotional—it contains some very beautiful passing tones. When I heard what he'd done with the arrangement, I had the impression that he was writing heartbreakingly beautiful stuff. It was a revelation to me—I never realized that Brian had that kind of talent for serious arranging before I heard this recording."

Here, Brian enhances the song's lyrical pensiveness by framing it in a semiclassical setting, using a string sextet and melancholic chords to cast a gloomy spell. Four violins, one viola, and a cello complement the melody; for these passages, he again highlights the dark, expressive tone of the lower strings—a sound favored by Johannes Brahms. "The string voicings on 'Don't Talk' are close, and he uses passing tones within diminished chords," explains violinist and string teacher, Nancy Ciminnisi. "When combined with the close harmonies in the lower register, this yields a rich, somber tone that meaningfully portrays the mood of the music. On this piece, Brian uses more violins, but the single viola takes the melodic lead. The low register instruments have the moving melodic line, while the violins sustain. He obviously wanted a certain texture and tone color, and the viola and cello brought that out."

The sustained tones double Brian's vocal lead, supporting the lines "Don't talk, put your head on my shoulder" and "Listen, listen, listen." These extended phrases are interpreted with ample vibrato, and, when combined with Brian's vaporous vocal lead, the foreboding attack of the timpani, and the soothing string ensemble, they emphasize the solemn tone. "Though he might not have studied Brahms or Ravel, he heard them in his head," said Phil Ramone. "That is evident in these chords, and the way they were voiced. It was unusual for pop music at that time. Because of Brian, John Lennon and Paul McCartney said, 'Jesus—we need something like that.' I can't help but think that he was worried about traditional record-company thinking: nobody wanted to change, and here he was thinking classically, which was a radical change. We don't live in a much different world today."

Another dazzling classical gesture comes during the album's pièce de résistance, "God Only Knows." Here, the French horn takes center stage, adding a euphoric air to the introduction. Alan Robinson, a 72-year-old veteran of the Utah Symphony and 20th Century Fox Studio Orchestra recalls the session in vivid detail. "I can close my eyes and see the inside of the recording studio," he says. "I was called at the last minute. 'Come right on down here and play,' they said. There was no music, and Brian sang the line to me, which was not a problem.

"I was sitting by myself with a baffle to my right; to my left side was the string section. Behind the string section was Hal Blaine; the percussion section was to his right, the guitars to his left. At eleven o'clock I could see the control booth. I'm visualizing all this now, 37 years later, and I've played thousands of sessions! I don't know why I remember it so well—I didn't even hear the record until years later. Maybe it's because I thought it was unusual that someone would sing something to me, and I'd have to play it."

In shaping the solo, Brian turned the commonplace into the sublime. "French horns are in the highest harmonic range, and because the notes are so close together and require smaller lip adjustments, you can do a sweep and cover all the harmonic tones between the five notes," Robinson explains. "That's why I was able to pass through the notes so quickly, and play those beautiful glissandos you hear on the introduction and the ending. Normally, I would have played a clean slur, but Brian came up with the idea of using a glissando."

There's much to admire in "God Only Knows." The song demonstrates how Brian perfected the use of chords and progressions; while all three verses are harmonically identical, the tonal center shifts around a bit—especially between the verses and the instrumental break or bridge. (These shifts are so understated that the listener is largely unaware of them.) Well-placed diminished chords also lend emotional emphasis to the song—in the phrases "you'll never need to doubt it" and "the world could show nothing to me," Brian uses a D-sharp diminished chord with an F-sharp in the bass. These chords and the passing tones and modulations he integrates throughout add color and reinforce the song's heavenly sound.

These effects were often fleshed out during the sessions, as the musicians worked through each part. "Music paper and chord sheets only give a musician the basics," says organist Larry Knechtel. "Brian would sit down and show us, because he had a lot of chords with different bass notes in the bottom, and inversions are difficult. 'God Only Knows' is very complex: he used a lot of moving bass lines and sophisticated harmony in that arrangement."

Carl Wilson agreed. "'God Only Knows' is the classic example [of Brian's writing] that takes it to a new plateau," he told David Leaf in 1996. "The bass wasn't played in the same key in which the song was written. It was inverted."

"God Only Knows" also highlights Brian's mastery of form. "The song demonstrates how well Brian understood the concept of 'theme and variation,' explains David Wright.

"The melody doesn't progress randomly: it keeps driving home a musical point. The French horn is heard at the beginning, and then repeats itself above his voice at the end. Its theme is reinforced throughout the piece. He understood that you don't make a musical point just once—you restate it a little differently each time."

In almost every situation, Brian made use of a favorite technique: doubling, in which two instruments play the same melody in unison. The process reinforces the structure of the melody, adds body and depth to the arrangement, and gives the final mix a spacious sound.

"Brian came up with new instrumental sounds by combining certain instruments," says Larry Knechtel. "He would use a grand piano, a tack piano, and a Wurlitzer electric piano—all playing the same thing. They were never exactly in tune, and it created a chorusing effect: a spatial phasing that they weren't able to get electronically."

Although the doubling of instruments was a technique that had been used for centuries (classical composers and orchestrators relied on it, especially those writing for woodwind, string, and choral ensembles), its application in modern rock music was largely limited to the doubling of electric bass. Brian revolutionized the technique by using it for virtually every instrument, from accordions to violins. The new sounds that he created were dynamic and bold, and became part of his distinct imprimatur.

"A lot of times Brian would 'sweeten' by having the guitars play together," says Jerry Cole. "Glen Campbell and I would play double acoustic 12-string sometimes—it gave us a big, round sound. On some sessions we'd have two acoustic, two electric, and two bass guitars. I would sometimes bring 13 or 14 guitars to the sessions—enough to fill two trunks. 12-string acoustic, six-string acoustic, third acoustic, a high strung electric guitar, a six-string bass guitar, eight-string electric basses—all different sounds and textures. Brian was like a kid in a candy shop! If he didn't like a particular sound, I'd say, 'Give me 30 seconds' and go grab another one."

Billy Strange remembers one impromptu session where he found himself without the guitar that Brian wanted. The overdub session—for "Sloop John B"—culminated in generous compensation. "I had recently divorced and was on the way out to pick up my son when Brian called and said he needed me right away," Strange says. "'Bring your son—maybe he'll enjoy it,' he said. When we got to the studio, he showed me a 16-bar solo he wanted me to play with an electric 12-string. I said, 'Brian, we have two problems. First, I don't have a guitar with me, and second, I don't even own an electric 12-string!'

"That didn't stop Brian. He called a friend at Wallichs' Music City in Hollywood, and in no time we had a 12-string and an amplifier in the studio. I plugged it in, tuned it up, and fiddled with it a little bit. Brian played the track for me, and we cut the solo in one take. Brian said, 'Great!' and handed me five hundred dollars. I was stunned. 'Brian, this is ridiculous for a 16-bar solo! He said, 'That's all right, Billy—and don't forget to take your guitar and amplifier with you.'"

Despite the Wrecking Crew's ubiquitous role on *Pet Sounds*, Carl Wilson's instrumental presence on the album was important to Brian, and he included him on "That's Not Me"—the only track on which any of the Beach Boys played.

"I remember playing 12-string direct, right through the board," Carl told David Leaf. "My playing wasn't as consequential as it had been before, and would later become, because everything had become more of an orchestra, part of a whole. It really wasn't appropriate for us to play on those [*Pet Sounds*] dates—the tracking just got beyond us."

The basic track was laid down by Carl (12-string guitar), Brian (organ), and Hal Blaine (drums). Although the specific recording dates and instrumentalists involved are vague, a number of other players overdubbed additional instrumentals after the primary session. "I distinctly remember that Terry Melcher played tambourine on that song," says Bruce Johnston. "Not long ago, he and I were listening to *Pet Sounds*, and he said, 'Gosh—this is such a great track, but the timing on the tambourine is off!' I said, 'Uh-hum. Terry, that's *you!*' He didn't remember it, but Terry Melcher is on the *Pet Sounds* album." (Melcher, a frequent visitor to Brian's sessions, was sometimes pressed into service as a percussionist. He is also listed on recording session contracts as having played tambourine on "Here Today.")

There's a decidedly southwestern approach to "That's Not Me," a sound reminiscent of the spacious atmosphere created by Aaron Copland for his imaginative ballets *Billy the Kid* and *Rodeo*. The uncluttered arrangement (featuring guitar, organ, bass, and percussion) allows each instrument to breathe, making the tune a study in contrast and texture. Here, the vibrancy of the bass stands out front and center.

Like many producers, Brian frequently doubled the electric and acoustic basses. "In the early '60s, there'd be as many as three basses on a record date," remembers Carol

Kaye. "Then, they narrowed it down to two. Lyle Ritz played string bass on practically all of the Beach Boys dates, and on some—like 'God Only Knows'—you can really hear him. Lyle used to kid that he was just 'ghosting' on the Beach Boy dates, but his string bass blended beautifully with my electric bass parts."

The mellowness of Ritz's acoustic bass softened the Fender's bite, adding discernible warmth. "I always tried to aim for a good resonance," Ritz says. "I would go for the satisfying resonance you get when you hit exactly the right note. When you hit it just right you can feel it through the seat of your pants."

"Sloop John B" is an excellent example of what Ritz describes. Together, the Fender and acoustic basses produce a fat, propulsive sound of unequaled clarity. Although few of the musicians knew it, Brian played Fender bass, which explains why it was emphasized on *Pet Sounds* "On the album, the Fender bass was used as an unveiled, prominent instrument—not in a supporting role, but as a prominent instrument heard in quiet, open passages," explains Bob Irwin. "All of the guitars and basses were being used in ways they'd never been used before."

The basses provided the solid framework that Brian desired. "Brian built a lot around Carol Kaye's bass parts," says Jerry Cole. "She was instrumental in building the foundation of so many of those records; her pick style and sense of time were excellent. Bass-wise, Lyle Ritz would play the foundation and Carol would play the lines."

Carol Kaye began her career in 1958 as a jazz guitarist, drawing on inspiration from Charlie Christian, the father of electric guitar. "I liked his style, especially his driving sound. It was a good, hard style, and that's how I always played, whether I was playing guitar or bass," she says.

Her use of a hard pick yielded a unique sound that Brian preferred. "[The bass] sounds much better with a pick," he explained. "It's more percussive. I wanted to have a 'pluck' sound like Motown, and I really liked the way Carol played." Kaye's unique sound can be heard throughout the album, especially on "I'm Waiting For The Day," where is it doubled against the oboe in the passage leading into the last chorus.

"I was one of the first players to use a pick on the bass in the studios," Kaye explains. "Ray Pohlman occasionally used one, but he played laid-back lines, and mostly with his thumb. Most producers liked the hard punchy sound I got with the pick, and many stopped using multiple basses. Brian would have me turn up the treble more than I normally would have on records where the deep bass parts sound like I'm playing with my fingers, and not the pick."

Pohlman can be heard on "I Just Wasn't Made for These Times," another tune with an interesting bass line. In the first part of each verse, the bass plays eighth notes (two notes per beat) in a register that was uncharacteristic for pop bass in 1966. "Most bass lines of the day employed simple foundational rhythms and root notes to outline the harmony and drive the rhythm section," says bass guitarist and music teacher, Amedeo Ciminnisi. "Brian departs from this by including a more involved rhythm in the verse—and using non-chord tones in the bass line." When the bass lays back later in the verse, the temple blocks add a different percussive flavor that picks up its busy rhythm.

Several interesting rhythmic bass patterns and devices also emerge on "Here Today." Throughout, the bass line accentuates the melody. The bass and horns also move in contrary motion to the vocals: in the chorus, the rhythm section and the horns play a descending line of quarter notes while the vocals ascend with "Ah-ah."

This break presents another neat rhythmic situation. The first eight measures consist of short, accented punctuations by all of the instruments except the pulsating bass. Two minutes and three seconds into the song a fascinating rhythm develops: all instruments (primarily piano and circus-style organ) maintain the tempo, but the feel changes when the snare pounds out a set of polka-like eighth notes. The final section features the organ playing quarter notes, while the bass and guitars play an ascending line in unison against the organ until they climax in a descending flurry of sixteenth notes.

The descending electric bass run becomes a focal point of the tune. "[On 'Here Today'] I wanted to conceive the idea of a bass guitar playing an octave higher than regular, and showcase it as the principal instrument in the track," Brian explained to journalist, Ken Sharp. A kick drum doubled with an open tambourine lends the recording a shimmering effect; the addition of a Four Seasons–style honking baritone sax line provides an unmistakable groove.

The *Pet Sounds* tracking dates were sessions the musicians looked forward to, because of Brian's professionalism and the sheer musicality of his melodies. "Brian had a means of pulling things together that wouldn't have seemed possible," says Billy Strange. "He didn't do what everyone else was doing, nor did he do what you'd expect. He amazed us; you didn't look at his music and say, 'Oh, I played something like that this morning on another session.' Everything that Brian did was off the wall—brand new—and we understood him. Of course, he had an advantage: he wrote the music. He built it from the ground up. Once he had the first eight bars of a song in his mind, the licks automatically fell into place. He played with it at home, he played with it while he was driving in the car, and when he walked into the studio Brian knew exactly what he wanted. All he had to do was record it."

When it came to closing *Pet Sounds*, Brian knew exactly what he wanted: a nonmusical tag to end "Caroline No"—and the album—on a sorrowful note. As the balmy warmth of the bass flutes and vibes bring the song to its conclusion, we hear two dogs barking as a train rumbles past, its lonesome whistle fading slowly into the distance. No one remembers how he came up with the idea, or where he found the train whistle. But the session at which Brian recorded his dogs (Banana and Louie) was surely the most bizarre that Chuck Britz ever supervised. "The dogs were sitting in the studio, and they were howling," he recalled. "We did this for six or seven hours. I kept the doors closed and said, 'Guys, please don't let the dogs outside of here.' But someone opened the damned double doors, and one of the dogs went roaming around. It walked up the stairs to where the men's room was, went into where they had an answering service, and pissed on about four people's legs! They finally came down and asked, 'Whose dog is that?' I said, 'It's not mine, but there's the guy.' I pointed to Brian, and he sent somebody to get it. I never did understand that session."

If bringing the dogs into the studio was perplexing, Britz was definitely unprepared for Brian's next request. Thinking it would make for a great album cover, he wanted to photograph a horse in Western Studio 3:

Brian: *Hey Chuck, is it possible we can bring a horse in here if we don't screw anything up?*

Britz: *I beg your pardon?*

Brian: *I want to get a picture of the horse in front of the microphone. Honest to God, the horse is tame and everything.*

Britz: *Just bring his trainer along behind him.*

Carl: *Brian, my horse would be so bitchin' in here.*

Needless to say, the whole idea was scrapped, no doubt much to Britz's relief.

Round Two: The Vocal Sessions

While the instrumental sessions created a vibrant foundation, capturing the group's spirited vocals on tape was a task that Brian Wilson enjoyed more than anything. When added to the melodies, they become *Pet Sounds'* defining element. "When you isolate the instrumentals on *Pet Sounds*, you realize that they weren't just conceived as music tracks that they would put voices on—they were constructed so as to work as a whole," says Tommy Morgan. "When I heard some of those instrumentals in the studio, I thought, 'Well, that doesn't sound all that good.' But when you hear them with the voices on, it's like, 'Oops! That's incredible.' There's a whole synergy that happens between what he conceived vocally and what he was doing instrumentally. The instrumental part was not complete without the vocals."

Although they appear breezy and carefree on the record, the *Pet Sounds* vocals were meticulously built in the studio, line by line. "Those vocal parts, and the recording of those vocal parts, are as fresh as planting a carrot and pulling it right up," says Bruce Johnston. "We didn't rehearse them prior to the session, and we didn't come back five days later to sing them. We learned the parts as we went along and put them right down on tape."

By the time the Beach Boys began recording *Pet Sounds*, it was rare for anyone except Carl to have heard the instrumental beds before the vocal overdubbing sessions began for a song. How did the rest of the Beach Boys react to first hearing the backing tracks for *Pet Sounds*? "[We were] dismayed—and that would probably be an understatement," said Al Jardine in Beach Boys fanzine *Beach Boys Stomp*. "We'd been traveling on the road, and when we came back, [we found] this incredible wealth of material, and it took us quite a while to adjust to it. We approached it like a job, but we had to be brought up to speed because it wasn't music you could necessarily dance to—it was more like music you could make love to. Like that great Moody Blues album *Days of Future Passed*, it had that kind of complexity to it, so it was quite a departure. Once we got the hang of it, it was magic."

To rehearse, they met at the studio, where Brian coached them in a football-style huddle around the piano. As with the instrumentals, he was explicit in delineating his desires. "Brian was like General Patton in the studio," says Johnston. "He was confident; he displayed a good sense of humor, and when necessary, strong leadership—which helped him accomplish his goal."

The vocal sessions often began in the afternoon and ran into the evening. "Usually, we'd be done early enough to hit the town and have dinner, or go to a club," Johnston remembers. "The prime destination in those days was the Luau, a fantastic watering hole on Rodeo Drive in Beverly Hills. If you looked old enough to drink they would serve you, and you could have some amazing Polynesian drinks there. It started out as a funky little bar when I was in high school, and turned into this wonderful Polynesian restaurant that *everyone* went to. Later, we might cross the street and go down to the Daisy to dance, or over to the Whisky on Sunset. We were very young guys with new money to burn. We all had young, gorgeous wives or girlfriends, and we weren't going to sit at home!"

Bruce Johnston, Al Jardine, and Mike Love all agree that unlike the instrumental tracking dates, the vocal sessions were anything but unstructured and free-wheeling. Although the same atmosphere may not have pervaded the sessions of the era's psychedelic and hard rock groups, the Beach Boys vocal sessions involved concentrated effort; decorum was the rule, not the exception. "Everybody dressed beautifully in those days," Johnston explains. "The questioning of authority hadn't really crept into society on a mass level; national drug use, beards and super-long hair and bell-bottoms hadn't taken root yet. We'd go to the recording sessions dressed a lot better than most people dress today, because that was the norm. I might show up in corduroy pants and a sweater and a button-down shirt, so you could go out after and look halfway decent on a weeknight. Those were wonderful times! You'd go to your job, which was to help Brian Wilson execute his magic, and then you'd end up at a club or the Luau and have a fabulous time."

Although he afforded his fellow band members some latitude, Brian usually had a specific, preconceived notion of what he wanted from them vocally. At no time were his thoughts more cogent or his expectations higher than during the *Pet Sounds* vocal sessions. "He was really pushing us toward greatness on *Pet Sounds*," says Mike Love. "He'd spend hours and hours honing a passage to perfection. We did one passage of 'Wouldn't It Be Nice' close to 30 times—and some of the tries were nearly perfect! But Brian was looking for something more than the actual notes or the blend: he was reaching for something mystical—out of the range of hearing. To our ears, it sounded great. But Brian thought it was off, so we did it again and again, until he was satisfied that we'd done it as well as we possibly could."

Love still marvels at his cousin's ability to think of multiple parts simultaneously. "When we were learning an arrangement, he would sit at the piano and 'deal out' the parts. He would sing the melody, or else the high falsetto part, but he would have all the parts in his mind—intricate parts that were moving all over the place. It was all you could do to learn your own part—but he'd have *four* of them in his head. That always kind of blew my mind, that Brian had that ability to hear all those parts at once, and parcel them out to each of us. It was a real gift."

On *Pet Sounds*, Brian used the vocal tone of each band member as he would any other instrument. "When Brian presented a song to us, we would almost know what our part would be," Carl explained. "Michael always sang the bottom, and I would sing the part above. Next would come Dennis or Alan, and then Brian on top. We had a feeling for it."

As always, Mike's doo-wop inflections added a meaty dimension to the vocal blend. "The bass is the root of four-part harmony, and it was artistically satisfying to add that," Love says. "I have resonance, but I don't have volume, so they gave me my own mike. I'd get that resonance going, and it would provide the deep, rich basis of the chords."

In addition to lending fullness to the bottom end, Love often penned words to Brian's melodies, and he contributed to the vocal arrangements as well. "It's not widely known, but Michael had a hand in a lot of the arrangements," Carl said in 1983. "He would bring out the funkier approaches. It makes a big difference, because it can change the whole rhythm—the whole color and tone of it."

Whether the net result was a full-blown, sun-drenched Beach Boys record or one of Brian's more serious compositions, the vocal recording formula used remained consistent with the well-established routine born of their earliest sessions. "All that had been worked out with the early hits," says Johnston. "Chuck Britz had it down—he knew how everyone sang, and what microphones needed to be put up in the studio. Singing in a small room was part of the magic, though not as important as what Brian and Chuck engineered."

Much later, in 1996, Chuck Britz recalled the vocal dates at Western Studio 3. "It was a beautiful sound," he said. "I could get beautiful tonalities out of them. They were six voices that blended beautifully, and Brian knew how to make their voices sound like instruments.

"It was a pleasure doing those sessions, because I didn't have that much work to do. A lot of times, Brian didn't tell me what everyone was doing. Not because he didn't want to, but because he was so wrapped up in thinking about what *he* wanted to do. Usually, Brian could hear right in the room what he wanted, and I could tell from the way he moved. It's surprising how well he could hear, being that he was singing lead vocals at the same time."

As with the instrumentals, doubling the vocal lead infused the harmonies with a reverberant glow. By recording a voice and then superimposing another voice over it, he added an airy dimension to the basic vocal track. "It strengthens the sound," Brian explained. "Sing it once, then sing it again over that, so both sounds are perfectly synchronized. This makes it much brighter, and gives it a rather shrill and magical sound without using echo chambers. It makes it sound spectacular—so much power."

"You can double the voices so four became eight; when harmonized by the same people, it sounds like twelve to sixteen voices," explains Phil Ramone. "Brian has that ability, so when you hear his voice doubled, it sounds immense. I recorded 'Wishing You Were Here' with Jimmy Guercio and Chicago in 1977, and Carl Wilson and some of the other Beach Boys did the background vocals. It was an amazing session. It's staggering when you hear four people stand up to a mike and sing beautiful harmony, but when you double it, it just goes into some other place."

As perfect as the Beach Boys' harmonies sound, their beauty actually lies in the imperfections. "In overdubbing a vocal line the second time, he wouldn't sing the part exactly the same way as the first one," explains musician and vocal music teacher Richard Battista. "He wouldn't care if it was a bit sloppy; he sang it that way purposely. The rhythm and pitch would be dead-on, but intonation-wise, it wouldn't match perfectly. When you put those two sounds together, it gives a fat 'rubbing sound'—the *chorusing* effect. Today, the effect is achieved electronically, but the results aren't nearly as pleasing as when the voice is singing it live, overdubbing to itself."

For the vocal sessions, the studio setup was not much different than it would have been 20 years earlier, when vocal quartets would band together around a single microphone. At that time, dynamics were achieved physically, not electronically. If the arrangement called for the emphasis of a certain voice or note, the member would close in on the microphone, later ducking aside to make way for another vocalist's entrance.

The microphone arrangement used for most of the Beach Boys sessions was straightforward. "We had two [Neumann] U47s, which Dennis, Carl, and Al would sing on, and a little cheap [Shure] 545 right in the middle," said Britz. "It was a very directional mike—I put a little filter on it. When Brian was doing his solos, he'd be on that mike and it sounded so great—fantastic! Every single song, Brian would always be on that mike. Then, he'd lean over and do background vocals with the guys—the four-part harmony."

Mike Love always had his own microphone, because his bass parts were almost inaudible without amplification. "He wasn't strong enough to cut through," explained Chuck Britz. "We kept him tight to the mike—a U47. That's how we got that deep sound." Often, Love's mouth would be pressed tightly against the capsule, and on more than one occasion Chuck Britz complained about him overloading the condenser mike's fragile diaphragm. "Every once in a while I'd say, 'Mike, would you please sing *across* the microphone instead of right into it?' He'd get upset, and say 'Aw, Chuck, why do you have to give me such a hard time?'"

After Bruce Johnston joined the band, the grouping of vocalists around the microphone changed. "When we were singing, Al would be on a little step, because Brian was so tall. Often, he [Brian] would have to spread his legs a little bit, to lower his height—so all of the sound could come evenly into the microphones," Johnston explains. "Brian had stopped touring, and I was filling in for him on the road. Before you know it, I was singing on the records. I was a fan way before that—and suddenly there I was, wearing a striped shirt on stage, singing Brian's high parts. But when I got into the studio and he said, 'Sing,' he did *not* have me sing his parts: he made an extra part for me. Brian realized he could have a new texture, just like another instrument."

Looking for variations in tone, Brian also experimented with microphone technique, as on "Wouldn't It Be Nice." "One of the features of this record is that Dennis sings in a special way, cupping his hands," Brian explained. "I had thought for hours of the best way to achieve the sound, and Dennis dug the idea because he knew it would work."

Vocally, the song took longer to track than any other *Pet Sounds* song. "'Wouldn't It Be Nice' presented a bit of a problem for Brian," explains Bruce Johnston. "Not vocally, but *rhythmically*. We couldn't execute the rhythmic parts of his arrangement for him, so we recorded it several times, and we even went out to his house, where he had a Scully four-track machine, to work on it. There are a lot of subtle rhythmic moves."

Many *Pet Sounds* songs highlight the involved rhythms built into Brian's vocal arrangements. For "I Just Wasn't Made for These Times," he created elaborate three-part vocal harmonies for the breaks. The vocals also supply rhythm, especially on the bridge, where the three-part vocal uses different melodies within the same chord structure:

Lead: "Sometimes I feel very sad."

Counter line 1: "Ain't found the right thing, I can sink my heart and soul into."

Counter line 2: "People I know don't want to be where I'm at."

Another interesting vocal study is "Here Today," which features an abundance of vocal weaving. Although most of the harmonies are limited to long-lined "Ooh-ooh's" and "aah-aah's," they provide a contrast in vocal texture. "The combination of wet and dry sounds on the vocals give it incredible dimension," says producer Phil Ramone. "What Brian does is superb: he hears a chord, he sings it, then works it in. There are harmonic structures that you don't normally hear within this production."

"Sloop John B" too is stunning. The production is replete with the glossy, multilayered vocalizing one expects on a Beach Boys record. As an unexpected twist, however, Brian dropped the instrumental completely from the bridge, letting the melody ride on a bed of a cappella vocal harmony—a trick that surprised everyone, including the band.

But the vocal summit of *Pet Sounds* occurs on "God Only Knows," on which Brian balanced music and voice to yield inspired, angelic tones of unsurpassed transparency. The performance is celestial, the harmonies as reverent as a Gregorian chant. But the purity of performance is a deceptive foil for the song's instrumental and vocal intricacy.

"'God Only Knows' is one of the Beach Boys' more innovative pieces of music," says David Wright. "It features counterpoint, and there's a lot going on vocally. They sing homophonically [with a single melodic line supported by chords], but there are many vocal parts, and a lot of interplay where voices are coming in and out at different times. It's much different than the background 'oo's' and 'ahh's' that they are noted for."

Brian originally sang the lead, but wisely chose to have Carl replace him. "Brian said something like, 'Don't do anything with it. Just sing it real straight. No effort. Take a breath. Let it go real easy,'" Carl told David Leaf in 1996. Bruce Johnston feels it was Carl's finest vocal performance. "Carl's vocal doubling is excellent—especially when he sings "O what good would living do me?" he says. "He goes up a major third there, and it's just as clean as a whistle."

At first, Brian planned to have a nonvocal bridge, and he overdubbed a saxophone solo for the break's second section.

Unhappy with the resulting mix, he scrapped the idea and created the vocal interlude that graces the final record. In the bridge's second section, the instrumental dissolves to a three-part vocal interlude, which is superimposed over bass, tambourine, wood blocks, violin, and cello. The beauty of this small but important section lies in the arrangement of its three different harmony parts, and the way those parts contrast and blend.

The primary vocal line features Carl, Brian, and Bruce singing a breathy, melodic "sigh"—a fluid phrase evocative of the French horn theme stated in the introduction. Superimposed over this are two lines: a series of syncopated "do-do-do-do-do-do-dos" and "ba-ba-ba-ba-ba-ba-bas" that provide contrasting rhythmic support. The interplay and blending of these separate vocal parts—sung by only three voices—is ingenious.

Then the "do-do-do-do-do-do-dos" that began as staccato notes swiftly merge into the overall "sigh" of the primary vocal, which forms the backdrop for the pulsating "ba-ba-ba-ba-ba-ba-ba" line. The tension builds, climaxing with a soaring glissando that resolves all three vocal parts to one single vaporous sigh—the most thrilling Beach Boys harmony on record.

Brian employs a clever musical device in this passage. The rhythmic nature of each vocal part conveys a sense of motion, finally culminating in the rhythmic unison of two half notes that bring the voices together. The effect of the opposing rhythmic elements merging provides a release in the tension—but not before a split second of suspense. "There's a jazz-inflected sound to the 'ba-ba-ba-ba-ba-ba-ba' part leading up to the sigh," explains Richard Battista. "That sigh is astonishing, and is totally unique in pop music. He didn't borrow that from the Four Freshmen, or the Everly Brothers, or the Coasters. That sigh is pure Brian Wilson."

Only one vocal performance rivals the interlude's intricacy and execution: the round-style ending tagged onto the song's final verse. According to Bruce Johnston, it is he and Brian who overdubbed the successive rounds, part by part.

"There are three voices sung by two people in the final part of the song: Brian, and me," he explains. "We were at the Columbia Records studio, overdubbing the vocals on an eight-track machine. After Carl finished singing the lead and center harmony parts he was tired, and Brian sent him home. But we had extra time—and open tracks. Brian and I stayed, and the two of us overdubbed additional vocal parts on the ending, with him singing the top and bottom parts, and me singing the middle. It works because it caused a perfect vocal-to-track balance, and it's not too top-heavy. It's brilliant—a fine example of 'less is more.'"

In this section, the third verse winds down and a prelude—played by the basses, violins, cellos, and wood blocks—introduces the finale. One at a time, the voices begin their entries, building to what sounds like a small choir chanting a mantra: "God only knows/God only knows/God only knows."

As the song concludes, the French horn returns, its mellow wail soaring high above the fray. Reaching for his falsetto, Brian parallels and echoes the instrument's lines on the words "without you," producing a seamless tapestry where instrument and voice melt into one. "The vocal overdubbing on the ending is extremely clean," says David Wright. "Brian's vocals are precise—it's part of what he wanted his voice to sound like. It's harder to distinguish who is singing when they overdub, because the process takes a bit of the personality out of the voice. But that was the effect he clearly wanted—it's part of what makes his voice sound so much like a French horn when he sings 'without you' at the end."

While the overdubs add depth and dimension (especially to the mono mix), it is musical craftsmanship that turns the short passage into a marvelous work of art. "There are lots of moving parts in the tag," explains Richard Battista. "The weaving, where it ends up blending and merging perfectly at the end, is extraordinary. Each vocal line is independent—it's not typical chime-up, block chord harmony. There are three or four melodic lines occurring simultaneously. There are chords within chords, and the chords change so fast that it's impossible to say at any given moment exactly what is happening chordally."

"If we were to freeze any given moment in that vocal tag, we'd likely hear a major-minor chord," believes David Wright. "Brian's music is so engaging because he took those major chords and put them together in interesting combinations. The harmonic progression in this section, and in the instrumental interlude is just captivating! When you build their harmony into those well-structured instrumentals, you immediately hear the key to their appeal."

The vocal sessions were inspiring. While they were initially put off by the new sound of Brian's music, the beauty of *Pet Sounds* wasn't lost on the rest of the band. As Carl Wilson explained, "The vocal parts on *Pet Sounds* were fascinating, so beautiful—and maybe mixed more subtly than some of our earlier records. It was during that time we had prayer sessions. It was very impromptu; Brian would actually write prayers down on paper. I remember being very impressed by that. I guess he wanted to see it, rather than just go inside himself. We prayed for guidance, to make the most healing sounds."

Post Production

Once the backing tracks and vocal overdubs were finished, all that was left to do was the final editing, mixing, and mastering of the record.

Because the vocals were added to a premixed mono instrumental track, mixing the album was easy. To create the two-track mono album master, Brian and Chuck Britz simply reduced the multitrack vocals to a single track and combined it with the mono instrumental track. A lack of paperwork precludes us from determining exactly where the album was mixed and mastered. It is likely, however, that half of it was mixed at CBS, the balance mixed by Chuck Britz at Western.

As mentioned previously, Columbia's eight-track recorder was the only such machine in town. Because their engineers were employees of the International Brotherhood of Electrical Workers union, strict rules would have prevented Britz—an outside recording engineer—from mixing from the eight-track tape machine at the CBS facility. That task may have fallen to Ralph Balantin, or another of Columbia's staff engineers who worked closely with Brian.

Overall, the original monophonic mix of *Pet Sounds* has a slightly overloaded, vacuum-tube compression sound—a quality that helps unify the individual recording elements.

Even though the instrumentals and vocals were recorded in multiple studios at different times, everything sounds as though it's coming from one place. During the mastering phase, equalization and compression were added to even out the sound.

Despite the care that Brian lavished on the recording sessions, the original mono version of *Pet Sounds* was not perfect. Whether a result of the era's technical limitations or the deadline imposed on him by the record company, the original mono mix he created is a bit sloppy, reminding us that it was a product of the imperfect analog heyday of classic rock 'n' roll. "I remember when Brian turned in *Pet Sounds*," said Steve Douglas. "It was full of noise. You could hear him talking in the background—it was real sloppy. He had spent all this time making this album and *zip*, dubbed it down in one day or something like that."

Although there is no reason to doubt its veracity, there is something unsettling about Steve Douglas's assertion, and this final stage of production. Why would Brian Wilson—a consummate professional who dedicated a significant part of his life to breaking boundaries and attaining perfection in the recording studio—settle for a less-than-perfect final mix? Why, after the meticulous hammer-and-tongs effort to construct a revolutionary masterpiece would Brian suddenly abandon his strong production values, and risk his considerable technical reputation? Could the deadline have been so inflexible as to prevent taking a bit more time to polish the final mix? Only two people could adequately answer these questions: Chuck Britz and Brian Wilson. Without their commentary, the best anyone can do is make an educated guess.

The technical limitations that Brian worked under certainly affected the quality of his final mix. He was pushing the technology to its very limits, in some cases mixing "on the fly" (recording an overdubbed instrument or vocal at the same time as he mixed other tracks down). If he were dubbing down "live" to mono, noises that would be difficult to correct later could easily have crept into the mix. In addition, he could simply have missed some of the noises and chatter, given the limitations of his hearing.

The most likely explanation, though, is that when it came to *Pet Sounds*, Brian felt that performance and feeling outweighed technical perfection. Like Phil Spector, Brian *felt* the music, and operated on gut instinct. If his goal were to create a specific "feel," he may have been oblivious to the inconsequential anomalies that were virtually undetectable on the playback equipment of the mid 1960s.

One of the most apparent technical flaws occurs up front, during "Wouldn't It Be Nice," where a noticeable intercut (edit) occurs on Mike Love's vocal entry in the bridge—the transition isn't smooth, and the volume suddenly spikes.

On "Here Today," we detect nonmusical anomalies, which are byproducts of the vocal overdubbing process. The most obvious occurrence happens between 1:52 and 1:56 (during the bridge), where some distant talking can be heard. It is the voice of Bruce Johnston. "When we were laying down the vocal on 'Here Today,' Brian yelled at me—and you can hear it on the track," Johnston explains. "It sounds like he's yelling at all of us, but I was the one talking. You can hear me talking, and Brian says, 'No talking!'—right during the instrumental. It was right before we were getting ready to sing, and I didn't think that Chuck Britz had pushed 'record.' I didn't think he was dropping it in until later."

"Caroline No" was altered by a technical slight of hand introduced during the mastering process. Following his father's advice, Brian sped up the recording, which raised the pitch of his voice one half-step to make it sound "younger." In doing so, the key of the song changed from C to C-sharp, and the tempo was increased accordingly. This technique ("Vari-speed") is commonly used for special effect, or to fine tune fixed pitch instruments such as xylophones, orchestra bells, and other instruments that cannot be tuned conventionally. The original tempo that Brian recorded the song in was slower, and better preserved the languorous, reflective tone of the song's subject.

Packaging Pet Sounds

Once the record was mixed and mastered, attention turned to the album's packaging. In an interview with David Leaf, Brian credits Carl with naming the album. But according to Mike Love, it was he who suggested the title *Pet Sounds*. "We were in the studio at Western one day, and from the hallway I could hear the passing train and barking dog that ended the album. I knew that Brian hadn't decided on a title yet, and after hearing those sounds, I said, "Why don't we call it *Pet Sounds?*"

In keeping with the theme, photographer George Jerman (himself a successful sound engineer and jazz record producer) took pictures of the band feeding animals at the San Diego Zoo. Although he sang on the record and was photographed with the group, Bruce Johnston is absent from the photo that appears on the album cover. "I'd been in the band under a year—I was the 'new guy,'" he says. "Also, I was still signed to Columbia Records, which meant my picture could not be on a competing album cover."

Regardless of who thought of it, there was no indication during the writing sessions that Brian was planning to call the album *Pet Sounds*. "Brian never mentioned anything about the album's title to me," says Tony Asher. "The first time I heard the whole album put together was during an evening at his house. He had some proofs of the pictures they'd done at the zoo, and he told me they were thinking of calling the record *Pet Sounds*. I thought it was a goofy name for an album—I thought it trivialized what we had accomplished. On the other hand, I was aware that many of Brian's off-the-wall ideas had turned out to be brilliant."

Did the odd title and incongruous photo leave people perplexed? Was it the cover that helped thwart album sales? The quirky title wasn't lost on Brian's colleagues, who drew their own conclusions regarding its meaning. "I think it's a vague, ambiguous title," says Jimmy Webb. "It's misleading when you look at the cover and see them feeding the animals at the zoo. What does 'pet sounds' mean? Animal sounds? Sounds for pets? What it became was *our* 'pet' sounds—the favored sounds of a generation of young people who were suddenly in the recording studio every day, working and making our living in there. *Pet Sounds* became our favorite record, and everyone picked up the torch and ran with it in his own way."

Not everyone appreciated the subtlety. "Paul McCartney and I spoke about the album in the spring of 1968, when we were in India together," recalls Mike Love. "In one conversation, he mentioned that we ought to take more care with our album covers. Paul was the mastermind behind the *Sgt. Pepper* album cover, which was detailed and brilliant. Ours . . . was a photo taken at the San Diego Zoo. That indicated how comprehensively Paul thought of everything. We didn't think about the packaging—we were never marketed thoughtfully, like the Beatles. That was partly our own fault, for not thinking as comprehensively as they did. I told Paul that we were more concerned with what was *inside* the album cover."

pet sounds **arrives**

"**Pet Sounds** was not a big hit. That really hurt Brian badly. He couldn't understand it. I think it had a lot to do with slowing him down."
Marilyn Wilson, 1976

"I've often played **Pet Sounds** and cried."
Sir Paul McCartney, 1996

Pet Sounds was released on May 16, 1966. Within two weeks it entered the charts at number 106. By July 2 it had peaked at number 10, remaining on *Billboard's* album charts for nearly 10 months. While it represented the most absorbing work they'd ever produced, it was the first studio album by the Beach Boys that failed to win a gold record award. It was also passed over at the 1966 Grammy awards, which was just beginning to recognize the rock 'n' roll genre.

It wasn't until 1966 that the National Academy of Recording Arts and Sciences began to take rock 'n' roll music seriously. The Beatles were ignored at the 1965 Grammy awards: an album of Henry Mancini songs by the Anita Kerr Singers won Best Performance by a Vocal Group over *Help!* However, the Fab Four hit two home runs in 1966, scoring big for "Michelle" (Song of the Year) and "Eleanor Rigby" (Best Contemporary Solo Vocal Performance). Ironically, the Anita Kerr Singers won again in 1966—for an album that included a cover of the Beach Boys' "Good Vibrations."

It was Frank Sinatra who swept the 1966 Grammy awards, winning Record of the Year and Best Male Vocal Performance for "Strangers in the Night." He also won Album of the Year for *Sinatra: A Man and His Music*. The Best Contemporary Recording was "Winchester Cathedral" by the New Vaudeville Band, and the song voted Best Contemporary Group Performance was "Monday, Monday" by the Mamas and the Papas.

Heading the list on the *Cashbox's* "Top 100 Albums" chart for 1966 were two film soundtracks (*The Sound of Music* and *Dr. Zhivago*), and three albums by Herb Alpert & the Tijuana Brass (*Whipped Cream & Other Delights*, *Going Places*, and *South of the Border*.) *Pet Sounds* charted at number 33, trailing *The Best of Herman's Hermits*, *The Best of the Animals*, *If You Can Believe Your Eyes and Ears* by the Mamas and the Papas, four albums by the Rolling Stones (*Big Hits*, *Out of Our Heads*, *Aftermath*, and *December's Children*), the Beatles' *Rubber Soul*, and the Dave Clark Five's *Greatest Hits*.

When the album received a lukewarm public reception, its creator wasn't surprised. Marilyn Wilson recently recalled the first time Brian played her the album, and his fretting over its seriousness. "Brian brought a copy of the album home when he was finished, and the first time I heard *Pet Sounds* was a special night. Brian was enthusiastic, and created a 'mood.' We were in our bedroom, and the lights were turned down low. He said, 'OK, are you ready?' He played it all the way through and it was one of the most moving experiences you could ever imagine. Brian was serious—it was like his soul was on that record. It was beautiful—one of the most spiritual moments of my entire life. We both listened and cried.

After the record finished, he said he was afraid that no one would like it—that it was too intricate."

The executives at Capitol were befuddled by the album, and they reacted with a halfhearted, self-serving promotional campaign. To ensure against total commercial failure, the label released *Best of the Beach Boys* shortly after *Pet Sounds*, effectively squelching any chance for the latter's success. As they predicted, *Best of the Beach Boys* topped out at number 8 within weeks, qualified for a gold record award, and remained on the charts for over a year.

What sparked Capitol's disdain for *Pet Sounds*? "I thought Brian was screwing up," asserted Nik Venet. "He was no longer looking to make records; he was looking for attention from the business. He was trying to torment his father with songs his father couldn't relate to, and melody structures his father couldn't understand." Brian found a sympathetic ally in Capitol's Karl Engemann. "I was with Brian when we went up to Capitol to play the album for Karl," says Mike Love. "He was a heck of a nice guy, and even though he liked *Pet Sounds* a lot, he asked if we couldn't make more records like the old [surf] stuff."

"I can remember when the album was delivered," Engemann told David Leaf in 1996. "On first listening, I knew it was different but it was so well done, and Brian was so enthusiastic about it—he was so in love with it—that you couldn't help but be excited.

"But then it was played at a sales meeting, and the marketing guys were really disappointed and down about the record, because it wasn't the normal 'Surfin' USA,' 'Help Me, Rhonda,' 'Barbara Ann' kind of production."

While Engemann may have been powerless to help in 1966, he was unwavering in his devotion to Brian and *Pet Sounds*. "In the 1960s, when the Beatles were at their creative and commercial peak, the Beach Boys were also right at the very top," he said. "And the music the Beach Boys made, particularly on *Pet Sounds*, was at the creative forefront of that whole period."

Pet Sounds was an anomalous Beach Boys album, which presented a perplexing situation for Brian, the band, and Capitol Records. With their solid body of hits tethered to surf, car, and girl themes, the label—and the public—had come to rely on them for a specific type of music. By 1965, their short but prolific reign as America's favorite group had been upset by the Beatles' descent on America. Keeping their readily identifiable sound front-and-center was essential, and *Pet Sounds* fell short of that mark.

To bolster its chance for success, the company insisted on including "Sloop John B," which had been recorded nine months earlier, on the album. Frothing over with requisite Beach Boys harmony, the tune made for a perfect single, and the label felt it would attract people to the more cerebral offerings on the album. While aesthetically questionable, the strategy proved sound. Released on March 21, 1966, the single (Capitol #5602) entered the charts on April 2, hitting the number 3 spot on May 7.

"Sloop John B" wasn't the first *Pet Sounds* single. "Caroline No" (Capitol #5610) was issued two weeks before, on March 7, 1966. The ruminating tune was the antithesis of "Sloop John B"—and most other familiar Beach Boys tunes. Heightening the boldness of its selection as the album's premiere single was its appearance as a *Brian Wilson* single—his first without the Beach Boys, and the only one issued during the Capitol era.

The solo designation was suggested by Steve Douglas. While it was intended to emphasize Brian's role in creating the album, it prompted the remaining Beach Boys to question whether he was poised to secede from the band. "I think they thought it [*Pet Sounds*] was for Brian Wilson only," Brian explained. "I think the problem was that they knew that Brian Wilson was gonna be a separate entity, something that was a force of his own. [But] they gave in to the fact that I had a little to say myself, so they let me have my stint. I told them it was only a temporary rift where I had something to say, and I wanted to step out of the group a little bit. And sure enough, I was able to."

Despite the beauty of Brian's new songs, the public thirsted for the familiar sound of the Beach Boys, and most of the tunes on *Pet Sounds* didn't fit the bill. Although it stayed on the *Billboard* Top 40 list for three weeks, "Caroline No" stalled at number 32.

The *Pet Sounds* single that captured the most attention was "God Only Knows," which was backed with the ebullient "Wouldn't It Be Nice" (Capitol #5706). Released on August 1, the record caused a stir in the radio community, where programmers were hesitant to promote songs with the word "God" in them. Although "God Only Knows" barely cracked the Top 40 chart (reaching number 39 in late September), "Wouldn't It Be Nice"—the "B" side—commandeered the lead, spending 11 weeks in the Hot 100 and peaking at a respectable number 8.

The failure of "Caroline No" to create a buzz raises an important question. Would *Pet Sounds* have fared better if it had been marketed as a Brian Wilson solo album? Probably not. If the public couldn't warm to an outstanding effort like "Caroline No" there is little reason to believe that a whole album—glorious as it may be—would have fared much better. Regardless, the issue of whether *Pet Sounds* is a Brian Wilson album or a Beach Boys album merits discussion.

If one views it from a participatory standpoint, the album is quite clearly a solo effort. Brian conceived, arranged, and produced the record, and, except for one track ("That's Not Me"), the Beach Boys made no instrumental contribution to it. Of the album's eleven vocal songs, Brian sang solo lead on five ("You Still Believe in Me," "Don't Talk," "I'm Waiting for the Day," "I Just Wasn't Made for These Times," and "Caroline No"). He also shares the lead on two ("Wouldn't It Be Nice" and "Sloop John B") and appears on the choruses of two more ("That's Not Me" and "I Know There's an Answer"). Brian sings for 16 of the record's 36 minutes (most of it lead); the rest of the Beach Boys sing for 13 of those minutes (much of it background).

But assessing the Beach Boys' importance to the album isn't that simple. Like it or not, in 1966 Brian—and *Pet Sounds*—needed the Beach Boys. At the time, Brian's "new" music was considered avant-garde, and, while he was admired and respected, Brian hadn't yet been widely hailed as the virtuoso that people now acknowledge him to be.

In branching off to write and produce *Pet Sounds*, Brian strategically employed the Beach Boys for three reasons: their talent, their brand recognition, and to maintain esprit de corps. Although it was Brian's brainchild, the appearance of the Beach Boys in name, performance, and spirit—however brief—helped afford *Pet Sounds* a credible identity, making it as much their album as Brian's.

British Reversal

While it received a tepid domestic reception, *Pet Sounds* made serious waves in Britain, where the publicist Derek Taylor, who worked with the Beatles and the Byrds, was engaged to promote the album. Beach Boy Bruce Johnston, the band's official emissary, nearly caused a riot when he hosted a star-studded listening party at London's Waldorf Hotel, which was attended by the Who's Keith Moon and Beatles John Lennon and Paul McCartney. "If I hadn't accidentally shown up in England, it would have probably been harder to launch *Pet Sounds*," Johnston believes. "Delivering Brian's masterpiece, and having the reaction of all the great artists and reviewers, made the label pay attention to what was happening in England. Ironic that in one part of the world [England] they were saying 'Hey, this is really great, Brian,' while in another part of the world [America] they were planning to release *Best of the Beach Boys*."

To mount the British campaign, Derek Taylor engaged the services of record producer-cum-diplomat Kim Fowley, who orchestrated the event as though it were the coronation of the Queen:

"I had known Bruce since 1956—we went to University High together. One day I got a call from Derek Taylor: 'Kim, I've got Bruce Johnston here in my office. I want you to make *Pet Sounds* gigantic in England. I want you to do your 'charisma shuffle,' and get everybody in the world to bow to Bruce Johnston. Get them excited about this album Brian has created called *Pet Sounds*.'

"There was no time to do research, so I said, 'Let's put him [Bruce] in an old-money hotel: a stodgy place, a traditional, old-school type place. Bruce would be the rock 'n' roll presence in the middle of all this stuffy British Empire architecture, which would be completely unexpected.

"We scheduled interviews so the journalists would see each other come and go. If one guy was to be there at eight and stay for an hour, we got the next guy to come at quarter to nine, so they'd see each other in passing and snarl. Most interviews were 15 minutes; some guys got an hour, depending on their rank. We wanted a horde of press, so it looked like the Beatles had just arrived at La Guardia Airport in 1964. Bruce Johnston was like Jesus Christ in tennis shoes, and *Pet Sounds* represented the Ten Commandments.

"We started at breakfast, and went well past the cocktail hour and into dinner. I wanted a big food budget, 'cause I wanted the press to eat better than they ever had before. People were all over the place—in the lobby, spilling out into the aisles and alcoves. The house detective was nervous. 'Are you smoking dope in there?' 'No, we're courting the British press, and we're playing music—at a reasonable volume!'"

As Fowley explains, his plan called for Johnston's connection with Who drummer Keith Moon, a colleague and fan of Brian's who could arrange for the presence of Britain's musical royalty at the party. The introduction to Moon came via Tony Rivers of the Castaways. "Keith was a good friend of mine, and wasn't yet the legend he came to be," Rivers says. "Surprisingly, Keith was a huge surf music fan, and loved the Beach Boys. I remember when he still lived in his parents' terraced house, and you'd walk down the street and hear *Shut Down, Vol. 2* blasting out of the window of the room that Keith and his wife shared in that house."

The night before the unveiling, Johnston attended a Who concert so he could meet Keith Moon. Sufficiently primed, Moon agreed to come to the album preview, promising to bring along two friends—Lennon and McCartney. Fowley describes the scene:

"The morning of the press party, I put Bruce in the presidential suite, and in comes Keith Moon—almost on cue. All the press guys began to buzz. 'Oh, the Merseys are here! We'd better not leave. Who's next? Marianne Faithfull! Oh my God—it's Marianne Faithfull, without Mick [Jagger].'

"Then came Dave Clark of the Dave Clark Five, and three or four members of the Beach Boys fan club. Finally, in walked John Lennon and Paul McCartney. When they did, the room stopped. I didn't stop—I cracked a joke. 'Oh, the big fish have arrived. This Hollywood shit works every time, doesn't it?' I knew that with John and Paul there, every moron out in the lobby was going to run back and report it, thereby anointing the project.

"John and Paul came dressed in Beatle gear—the same suits they wore in *Help!* No bodyguards, no wives, no Brian Epstein or George Martin—just the two of them in full Beatle regalia. The boots, the shirts, the hair. They moved quietly, like Ninja shadows, saying, 'Hello, everyone—you know us.'

"I asked Paul if they'd like anything to drink. 'Rum and coke—two, please.' The order was placed. 'Anything else?'

'Yes,' Paul said. 'We'd like a piano brought in.' I don't know where they got it, but an old upright quickly materialized. The fan club girls were off to the side playing cards, and Paul sauntered over. 'Oh, I know canasta—it's a game I played with my mother. Girls—I'm the dealer. John and I will sit here quietly and play cards, but I have another request: please don't talk during the album. John and I have to go over to Abbey Road when this is over, and we'd really like to listen to every track, and digest it. Is that OK with everyone?'

"The phone came off the hook, the needle went down, and we played the record all the way through. Not a word was spoken. Paul dealt the cards, everyone nodded and smiled, enthralled by what they were hearing. It was pandemonium out in the lobby, because not only were the other rock stars in there [the suite], but Lennon and McCartney were in there too. The press guys couldn't believe that the real Beatles were there. They must have been pressing against the keyhole—I'm sure they had glasses against the wall, trying to listen in.

"After the record was over, John and Paul jumped up and went to the piano. They each put their hands on the keyboard, plucking out some chords as they whispered to each other. Then, Paul rose, looked around the room, and bid everyone a farewell. 'Thank you very much—it's been a great visit. Sorry we can't spend more time, but we have studio time waiting. Say hi to Brian and Derek Taylor. Goodbye.'

"Gone. The room stopped after they left. Watching those guys listen to music was quite a treat—it was like being in a college classroom. What they were doing was memorizing the entire record, listening to the techniques used and Brian's musical point of view: the voicings, counterpoint, dynamics, and tuning. No notes were taken, and nothing was played again. They weren't there to pay tribute to Brian Wilson or Bruce Johnston; they were there to see what the competition was. They were there to take the best of *Pet Sounds* and apply it to *Revolver*, which they were recording at the time. They didn't steal lyrics, or notes, or chords. They stole emotional impact and pathos. They noticed how Brian got it, and decided it was OK to improve upon it, and have a song on *Revolver* that reflected the objective sensitivity that Brian had achieved with *Pet Sounds*."

The Waldorf preview may not have been the first time McCartney heard *Pet Sounds*. According to Rolling Stone's producer Andrew Loog Oldham, producer Lou Adler played McCartney a test pressing of the album before the press preview. "After *Pet Sounds* was released, Paul McCartney came to my house from London Airport. I sat in smoke with him, and that first listen changed our lives." Regardless of when or where the Beatles heard the album, it affected them.

Brian never forgot the role that Derek Taylor played in making *Pet Sounds* a hit in Britain. "When I first met Derek in 1966, I was immediately impressed by his great mind and his fantastic wit," Brian said on Taylor's death in 1997. "Derek had as much to do with the success of *Pet Sounds* and 'Good Vibrations' in England as anybody, including me, and for that alone I'm forever indebted. Despite what he wrote about me, it was Derek Taylor who was the genius. *He* was a genius writer. Derek was the one who came up with the term 'pocket symphony' to describe 'Good Vibrations.' He encapsulated the record perfectly! I admired the way he could express things."

The Beatles Redux

The correlation between *Pet Sounds* and *Revolver* is key to understanding the relationship between the Beatles and the Beach Boys. Recorded almost concurrently, the albums represent the bands' nexus, and, although they worked in isolation on different continents the two groups achieved an unusual synchronicity. There are many similarities—lyrical, instrumental, and technical—between the two albums.

Understanding the chronology is important. *Pet Sounds* was released on May 16, 1966. Less than one month after Brian Wilson and the Beach Boys completed the final sessions for the album at Western 3 and Gold Star in Hollywood (March 1966), the Beatles commenced with their first sessions for *Revolver* at Abbey Road Studios in London. Recorded between April and June, *Revolver* was released on August 5, 1966—a day that found Brian's "Wouldn't It Be Nice" firmly entrenched in the Hot 100 chart.

Without knowing the time line, one might believe that Brian's arrangements for "Don't Talk (Put Your Head on My Shoulder)" and "God Only Knows" inspired the elegiac string quartet backing for "Eleanor Rigby." And the Beatles' "Got to Get You into My Life" bears a striking rhythmic similarity to the spirited, toe-tapping feel of "Wouldn't It Be Nice." An excellent example of the similarity of the groups is apparent on the Beatles' "Here, There, and Everywhere," where the harmonies—especially the background vocals with the thick "ooh's" and "aah's"—feature similar modulations. "The harmonies on that are very simple," said Beatles producer George Martin. "Just basic triads—no counterpoint, just moving block harmonies. Very simple to do, but very effective." "This really is the first hint that the Beatles had picked up on what the Beach Boys were doing," believes Beatles historian Tom Frangione. "This song is a definite nod to the Beach Boys—something we hear both vocally and in the structure of the verses."

Instrumentally, the rhythm section on "Here, There, and Everywhere" is understated: muted tom-toms, brushed cymbals, closed high-hat, and a simple, melodic bass line—all dynamic techniques used to great effect in Brian's arrangements. Compositionally, the form (specifically the structure of the verses) is a nod to Brian's mid-'60s style, a method of song-writing that shunned the traditional A-A-B-A pattern of most pop songs in favor of unusual verse/chorus combinations.

In 1995, McCartney expressed his fondness for *Pet Sounds* on his *Oobu Joobu* radio series. "I was very impressed with a Beach Boy record called *Pet Sounds*," he said. "It was always one of my favorite albums—it still is in many ways. The writing that Brian Wilson did on that was really very special, I thought. I love his instrumentation, the melodies he wrote, and the harmonies he put with it. There's one that really gets to me, 'You Still Believe in Me.' I just love the big block of harmonies."

In an interview with David Leaf, McCartney amplified his affinity for the album. "*Pet Sounds* blew me out of the water. First of all, it was Brian's writing. I love the album so much. I've bought my kids each a copy of it for their education in life—I figure no one is educated musically 'till they've heard that album. I was into the writing and the songs.

"The other thing that made me sit up and take notice was the bass line on *Pet Sounds*. There's a kind of tension created.

I don't really understand how it happens musically, because I'm not very technical musically. But something special happens. Brian would be using notes that weren't obvious notes to be using, and also putting melodies in the bass line. That, I think, was probably the big influence that set me thinking when we recorded *Sgt. Pepper.*"

As early as *Revolver*, we hear a new complexity in McCartney's bass playing—a factor he freely attributes to Brian. "Brian Wilson was a big influence," McCartney said in Mark Lewisohn's *The Beatles Recording Sessions*. "Strange, really, because he's not known as a bass man. If you listen to *Pet Sounds*, there's a very interesting bass—it's nearly always a bit offbeat. If you've got a song in C, the first bass note will normally be a C. But his [Brian's, as played by Carol Kaye or Ray Pohlman] would be a G. He'd put the note where it was not supposed to be. It still fit, but it gave you a whole new feel. I'll never forget putting the bass line in 'Michelle,' because it was kind of a Bizet thing. It really turned the song around. You could do that with bass—it was very exciting."

Another unusual sound caught McCartney's ear. "On *Pet Sounds*, there's a lot of harmonica—bass harmonica. It's the instruments he uses, and the way he places them against each other. It's a really clever album. We were inspired by it—and nicked a few ideas."

Mike Love recalls an occasion when McCartney shared his love for *Pet Sounds* with Brian himself. "We were at a birthday party for Carl at his Malibu beach house," Love says. "Paul was there with Linda, sitting on the sofa. During the evening, he turned to Brian, and said, 'Hey Brian, I was driving across Mulholland Drive this morning, playing

Pet Sounds in the car, tears comin' out of my eyes. Brian, when are you going to give us another *Pet Sounds?'* That tells you how much Paul is emotionally affected by the album, because he's a musician and is able to recognize that genius in someone else's work."

The cross-pollination that began with *Rubber Soul* continued as the Beatles extended the epic rock album concept with the June 1967 release of *Sgt. Pepper's Lonely Hearts Club Band,* an album that both George Martin and Paul McCartney admit was greatly influenced by *Pet Sounds.* "I believe that without [Brian's] inspiration, *Sgt. Pepper* might have been less of the phenomenon that it became," Martin explained. "Brian Wilson is . . . a living genius of pop music. His invention and creativity reached a level that I always found staggering. He gave the Beatles and myself quite a good deal to think about in trying to keep up with him. And like them, he pushed forward the frontiers of popular music. His art is that magical combination of really original compositions, a wonderful sense of instrumental color, and a profound understanding of record production."

Although Brian himself doesn't see the parallel ("These two albums aren't very alike at all—they must have picked up on the creativity of *Pet Sounds,* not the sound"), several moments on *Sgt. Pepper* illustrate the influence.

"She's Leaving Home," a ballad comparable in spirit to "Don't Talk (Put Your Head on My Shoulder)" or "Caroline No," could have easily been a Brian Wilson song written for *Pet Sounds.* Like "Don't Talk . . . " the instrumentation is sparse, featuring a lone harp and string quartet. Ethereal background vocals (tape-doubled and sung in overlapping rounds) add to the pensive mood of the lyric. (The song was recorded in sections, with each chorus edited together for the final mix— a technical manipulation that heightens the tension.)

"Within You Without You," a largely instrumental track featuring sitar, percussion, and strings, is reminiscent of the rhythms and instrumentation of the song "Pet Sounds," although George Harrison surely drew on his love of Indian music in composing the Beatles track.

More to the point, "With a Little Help from My Friends" is urged along by yet another of McCartney's relentless, tuneful bass lines which was surely encouraged by Brian's style. "Paul didn't start using the upper register of his Rickenbacker bass until after he heard *Pet Sounds*," explains Beach Boys historian Lenie Colacino, a musician who played in *Beatlemania*. "The bass parts that Brian wrote for 'Here Today' directly influenced the way Paul played on 'With a Little Help from My Friends' and 'Getting Better.'"

In "Getting Better," the bass is taut, focused, and melodically voiced. Here, Lennon and McCartney incorporated unconventional rhythmic changes—one of Brian's favorite compositional tricks. The background harmonies (while meager compared to the plush Beach Boys sound) project tightly interlocked chords.

The Beatles and George Martin also mimicked the heavy percussion (timpani and floor toms) so prevalent throughout *Pet Sounds*; the effect is evident on "Sgt. Pepper's Lonely Hearts Club Band," "With a Little Help from My Friends," and "A Day in the Life."

The greatest effect that *Pet Sounds* had on *Sgt. Pepper*, however, was in its intellectual approach. "With *Pet Sounds*,

Brian had stepped outside of the band, yet still called it the Beach Boys," explains music historian Jon Butcher. "It demonstrated to McCartney that the Beatles did not have to be confined within the Beatles, and indeed, McCartney's idea was to assume another identity on *Sgt. Pepper*." George Martin agreed, confirming that "Paul said, 'Why don't we make the whole album as though the Pepper band really existed—as though Sergeant Pepper was doing the record? From that moment on, it was as if *Pepper* had a life of its own."

In truth, Brian's aborted *Smile* recordings may have had the most influence over what the Beatles wrought with *Sgt. Pepper*. "The year before *Sgt. Pepper*, the Beatles had gone to Los Angeles to listen to the eight-track *Smile* sessions, and what they were looking for is revealed on that album," explained lyricist Van Dyke Parks in a 1999 interview with Will Hodgkinson of *The Guardian*. "It was improper for the Beatles to take the musique concrète approach that Brian had started, and it was grievous because they were so obviously better than that."

Whether *Pet Sounds* or *Smile* egged the Beatles on or not, *Sgt. Pepper* captured Brian's ear. "The Beatles did *Sgt. Pepper's Lonely Hearts Club Band*, and I said, 'There's their creative explosion,' he recently explained. "They exploded in creativity. I guess *Pet Sounds* really got to Paul and John, you know. I was blown out! I couldn't believe it. [It] just absolutely flipped me out. Some of their stuff was scary, like the very ending of 'A Day in the Life' [the prolonged, ominous piano chord]. That sounded like doom to me—like the end, you know?"

The effects of *Pet Sounds* on the Beatles reverberated well past the 42-second E major chord that closes *Sgt. Pepper*. By the time the Beatles finished *Magical Mystery Tour*, it was clear they'd fully assimilated the essence of Brian's eclectic arranging style, and they volleyed it back within songs like "Hello, Goodbye," "The Fool on the Hill," "Your Mother Should Know," and "Penny Lane." (The released version of "Penny Lane" features a distinctive brass section and strings; an earlier, unused mix featured an oboe instead of the brass. The pairing of oboe and strings makes the song sound as though Brian had written it himself.)

Both the Beatles and the Beach Boys saw their art rise to unprecedented heights during the mid-1960s. The inter-band competition was friendly and stimulating; it—like the music—fostered mutual growth.

Stellar Support

In addition to the Beatles and Keith Moon, many British rockers marveled at Brian's achievement. "All of us—Ginger [Baker], Jack [Bruce], and I consider it to be one of the greatest pop LPs to ever be released," said Eric Clapton (then a member of Cream) in 1966. "It encompasses everything that's ever knocked me out and rolled it all into one. We're all gassed by it. Brian Wilson is, without a doubt, a pop genius."

Andrew Loog Oldham likened the record to Rimsky-Korsakov's *Scheherazade*. "*Pet Sounds* changed my life for the better. On the personal side, it spoke for me when I was too busy to have a personal life. The sound and music—the words of Tony Asher blended into the melodic slices of Brian Wilson—spoke of pain and coming of age in a way that allowed young ambitious dudes to let him speak for us whilst we hid whatever and hung tough. It was my 'primal scream.'"

The British press also embraced the album, their top music critics penning glowing reviews. "Just out in America is a brand new spanking hot Beach Boys LP called *Pet Sounds*," wrote Penny Valentine in *Disc and Music Echo*. "Thirteen tracks of Brian Wilson genius . . . each track has that lovely, distinctive smothered Wilson sound—as though they're all singing through sugar cotton wool. The whole LP is far more romantic than the usual Beach Boys jollity: sad little wistful songs about lost love and found love and all-around love."

Topping it all off, the year's end saw the Beach Boys edge out the Beatles in a British popularity poll—a fact trumpeted in the December 10, 1966, edition of the *New Musical Express*: "Show business will vibrate with the sensational news that the Beatles have been outvoted by the Beach Boys as the World's Outstanding Vocal Group!"

With its marvelous British reception, why was the beauty of *Pet Sounds* lost on American audiences, critics, and label executives? To understand the commercial failure of *Pet Sounds* on its initial release, we must consider the state of the record industry in 1966.

At that point, teenagers—the real record buyers—quenched their musical thirst with 7-inch, 45-rpm singles priced under a dollar. Unlike their parents, few youngsters purchased LPs, and AM radio encouraged the sale of singles by featuring the top hits, which were conveniently divided into 'A' (the choice cut to be plugged by the radio disc jockeys) and 'B' sides. (That's not to say that albums weren't plugged; once the Beatles hit the United States, AM stations—the radio outlets that only played 45-rpm singles—began spotlighting LPs. Often, Top 40 stations would feature an "Album of the Week" and play individual cuts hourly during their daily rotation, giving the entire album tremendous exposure by the week's end.)

Perhaps the world just wasn't ready for *Pet Sounds*, a serious album by a surf band that arrived on the brink of a revolutionary period in modern popular music. The folk- and protest-inspired music of the Vietnam era was taking root, the "Summer of Love" was still a year away, and teenagers still possessed a palpable innocence, craving three-minute dance tunes that reflected the carefree essence of youth. *Pet Sounds* presented something quite different to what Beach Boys fans had come to expect from the band, and like the mighty, dissonant symphonies of Mahler and Shostakovich the music required an open mind and a willingness to engage in active listening. Sadly, few people invested the time or effort, and it would be 30 years before *Pet Sounds* was recognized as a paragon of rock 'n' roll finesse.

In 1967 Brian acknowledged the public's changing perception of the group and its music. His statement reflects acceptance, but the subtext reveals his disappointment over the commercial failure of his masterwork. "I know that in some circles we're not regarded as 'hip' or 'in,'" he said. "But I don't care too much what anyone says, so long as I'm staying ahead—right up to the limit of my present capabilities. I don't put out anything I don't respect. And I know for sure that the Beach Boys brought something new to rock 'n' roll."

brian's in-between years (1967–1990)

"When people think of the Beach Boys, I would like them to think of 'Good Vibrations.'"

Brian Wilson

Before completing *Pet Sounds*, Brian began studio work on the album's follow-up, a record he freely asserted would be better than its predecessor. "I'm writing a teenage symphony to God," he explained. He initially called the project *Dumb Angel*, but it was later renamed *Smile*. Supplanting Tony Asher was Van Dyke Parks, a mild-mannered intellectual who shared Brian's grandiose vision.

Parks, who met Wilson in 1965, is a multitalented musician, producer, and arranger. His first studio assignment was arranging "The Bare Necessities" for Walt Disney's *The Jungle Book*; soon after he was working with the Byrds, the Fifth Dimension, Ry Cooder, Randy Newman, and Judy Collins.

Why didn't Brian continue his association with Asher, a lyricist he admired and with whom he'd just completed a groundbreaking album? "With 'Good Vibrations' finished, I picked up work again with Van Dyke Parks, to the disappointment of Tony Asher, who'd done a great job on *Pet Sounds*," Brian explained. "But I chose collaborators by intuition—by the vibes I got from them—and Van Dyke's intellectual passion and esoteric way with words seemed to mesh with the way I was feeling. We were completely different individuals, yet, with amphetamines pushing a freight train of ideas through our brains, Van Dyke and I enjoyed a compatibility that was inspiring."

Asher never expected the call to write *Pet Sounds*, let alone another album with Wilson. "The notion that I would continue to write with Brian never came up and frankly, I wasn't surprised," Asher says. "Remember: *Pet Sounds* was considered a flop. Even before the songs were recorded, I knew that the rest of the group felt that Brian's decision to write with me was a bad decision. So, it would have been pretty gutsy of him to say 'I don't care what you guys think,' or 'I don't care if you *were* right about *Pet Sounds*, I'm working with this guy anyway.' At that point, he wasn't secure enough. Then, he may have had doubts about whether I had been the right choice, but that's just a guess on my part."

Smile

The *Smile* album represented the height of poetic lyricism— it was a finely chiseled study in texture and contrast. Although many feel that the song "Heroes and Villains" is the key to understanding the album, it is "Good Vibrations"— which was taped between the sessions for "I Just Wasn't Made for These Times" and "God Only Knows" in February and March 1966—that everyone remembers. The three-minute, thirty-five-second track, which was spliced together from separate parts recorded in several studios, redefined the production of pop music, and of singles in particular. "I'm most proud of 'Good Vibrations,'" Brian said in 1966. "It exemplifies a whole era. It's a whole, involved piece of music that says something."

Entire books have been written about the complicated history of *Smile*, and its psycho-emotional significance in the Wilson canon. In short, the *Smile* sessions represent the last vestiges of Brian's musical prescience. While *Pet Sounds* was responsible for Brian's emergence in a new arena, the *Smile* project—and his relentless use of drugs—hammered him into hell, devastating his psyche. The wounds were deep, and Brian never fully recovered.

Brian's bizarre comments reflected an increasing paranoia. "Spector started the whole thing," he explained to Jules Siegel in *Cheetah* magazine in 1967. "He was the first one to use the studio. But I've gone beyond him now. I'm doing the spiritual sound—a white spiritual sound. Religious music. Did you hear the Beatles album? Religious, right? That's the whole movement. That's where I'm going. It's going to scare a lot of people."

When a fire broke out near the Los Angeles recording studio in which he was taping "Fire" (part of a longer suite titled "The Elements") it was Wilson who ran scared, believing his music possessed telepathic powers capable of provoking the wrath of God.

In the *Cheetah* article, Siegel (who attended the *Smile* sessions) detailed Brian's increasingly odd behavior. "As the year drew deeper into winter, Brian's rate of activity grew more and more frantic, but nothing seemed to be accomplished. He tore the house apart and half redecorated it. One section of the living room was filled with a full-sized Arabian tent, and the dining room, where the grand piano stood, was filled with sand to a depth of a foot or so and draped with nursery curtains. He had had his windows stained gray and put a sauna bath in the bedroom."

In the studio, he worked feverishly to accomplish what some believed was a futile goal: perfection. There were sensational reports that Brian lit small bucket fires in the studio to enhance the infernal atmosphere the "Fire" melody depicted. According to the musicians present, however, this never occurred. "Brian was way too professional for that," says Carol Kaye. "He did bring some plastic fireman hats to Gold Star, but Lyle Ritz was the only musician who wore one. I distinctly remember the 'Fire' sessions because I was amazed at how Brian got the cellos to sound like real fire engines."

Also suspect is Wilson's reported claim to have personally destroyed the *Smile* tapes. A thorough search of the tape vaults (conducted by engineer Mark Linett and Wilson's friend Andy Paley in the late 1980s) yielded a substantial amount of *Smile* material, much of which has reached the collector's market on high-quality bootlegs.

While it was thoroughly unconventional, the music composed for the album was compelling, and many of the musicians had trouble seeing where *Pet Sounds* left off and *Smile* began. "Brian was growing very fast, and *Smile* was his greatest work—even better than *Pet Sounds*," Kaye believes.

Why did this breakthrough album remain unfinished? Some speculate it was because of Brian's downward emotional spiral; more likely, it was a legal dispute between the Beach Boys and Capitol Records over royalties that delayed its completion. For whatever reason, Brian lost interest in the project, and the world lost a brilliant sequel to *Pet Sounds*. "*Smile* promised to be a major breakthrough in popular music, what might be called 'modular' music. And, as 'Good Vibrations' had, *Smile* would have taken Brian Wilson's artistry to a new level," believes David Leaf. "But what *Smile* might have been was what the absence of *Smile* came to represent. In essence, the end of work on *Smile* was the public evidence; what we wouldn't come to fully understand for a long time was that it represented the artistic repression of Brian Wilson. It was a time when Brian ignored all the limits and the boundaries as an artist, and was operating in another area of consciousness. For a brief time, he captured all of it in his music. But when you're on the edge, you need to know that if you jump, somebody will catch you. And sadly, despite all he had accomplished as an artist, he just didn't have that kind of support in his life."

As Brian's concepts, music, and lyrics veered further astray so did his mental state. The weight of the *Smile* sessions and the criticism of the music by his band mates sent him into depression. The erratic behavior first exhibited in late 1964 returned, and in the spring of 1967 he retreated, leaving the rest of the Beach Boys to fashion a makeshift album from the *Smile* sessions.

After Smile

With *Smile* died the promise of Brian's most anticipated musical moment, leaving him disillusioned and drained. After *Smile*, his drug use escalated; the monstrous chemical cocktail now included hash, LSD, cocaine, amphetamines, and alcohol. Even so, there were some notable (if not quite triumphant) post-*Smile* moments.

Public perception worsened when the Beach Boys declined an invitation to perform at the 1967 Monterey Pop Festival. Their rejection was understandable: disciples of San

Francisco's flourishing psychedelic music scene viewed their non-rebellious, apolitical reputation with condescension. As war raged in Vietnam, rock musicians took a hard stand, speaking out against the government in words and music. Caught between the Mamas and the Papas, the Byrds, Jimi Hendrix, the Doors, the Beatles, and Jefferson Airplane (and roundly criticized in San Francisco's music journal *Rolling Stone* magazine), the Beach Boys retreated, taking a back seat to the musical and political vortex swirling around them.

In September 1967—three months after the Monterey withdrawal—the band released *Smiley Smile*. Of the twelve original *Smile* tracks, five were included on the revised album. Only two resembled Brian's original concepts, and, in light of *Smile*'s high expectations, the substitute album failed to sate the appetite of the Beach Boys' staunchest fans. Even Carl Wilson was disappointed, saying that *Smiley Smile* "was a bunt instead of a grand slam."

Wild Honey (released just three months after *Smiley Smile*) signals an admirable return to both the R & B roots of their youth and a simpler method of recording. Lacking the finesse of *Pet Sounds* (and almost every trace of traditional Beach Boys harmony), *Wild Honey* has a raw, funky edge that's reminiscent of the Rolling Stones and Sly & the Family Stone.

The album, which was recorded at Brian's home studio with the members playing their own instruments, allowed the band the opportunity to regroup and to reassess its place in rock music. The commercial success of "Darlin'" (which topped out at number 19 on the charts) and the presence of several outstanding tunes ("Let the Wind Blow," "Here Comes the Night," and "Wild Honey") notwithstanding, the album missed the mark. But if *Wild Honey* represented the band's 1960s nadir, its follow-ups—*Friends* and 20/20—marked its artistic revitalization.

On *Friends*, the Wrecking Crew returned, and the recordings possess the exceptional production values that began with *Pet Sounds*. Unlike *Wild Honey*, the songs and their arrangements are inspired, and, given the pro-peace movement of the late 1960s, relevant. "The songwriting cycle for *Friends* came quickly to me," Brian said. "The bad things that had happened to me had taken their toll, and I was free to find out just how much I had grown through the emotional pain that had come my way." The album is one that Brian, for a time, called his favorite. "It seems to fit the way I live better," he said after it was released. "It's simple, and I can hear it any time without having to get into some mood. *Pet Sounds* carries a lot more emotion—at least for me. [*Pet Sounds*] is by far our best album. Still, though, my favorite is *Friends*."

20/20 extended what had begun with *Friends*, bringing the Beach Boys full circle. From the opening track ("Do It Again"), the vitality of the band's early '60s recordings resurfaces, and the record contains many delightful surprises. The album marks the production debuts of both Carl Wilson and Bruce Johnston. (Carl would go on to fully produce the band's version of Phil Spector's "I Can Hear Music"—first recorded and released by the Ronettes in 1966—while Johnston would go on to produce the cover of Ersel Hickey's "Bluebirds Over the Mountain"—first recorded and released in 1958 on Epic Records.) Several songs here (including the mesmerizing "Our Prayer") are standouts, but it is Johnston's eloquent "The Nearest Faraway Place"—a statement of his love for *Pet*

Sounds—that proves to be the album's prettiest song. Like *Friends*, 20/20 is solid, and many of its songs—especially their cover of Leadbelly's "Cotton Fields"—are evidence of what the Beach Boys should have done on *Wild Honey*.

Despite the soundness of both *Friends* and 20/20, the public voted "no." "Do It Again" reached number 20 (their last Top 20 hit of the '60s), but both albums fared poorly on the charts, peaking at numbers 136 and 68 respectively.

Till I Die: The 1970s

1970 saw the release of the band's first Brother Records label effort, *Sunflower*, a sparkling album that features the infectious "Add Some Music to Your Day" and Brian's beautiful "Cool, Cool Water." In 1971, Brian produced several singles and an album for wife Marilyn and her sister Diane Rovell, who performed in a band formerly known as the Honeys. The album was called *Spring*, the name that Marilyn and Diane adopted for themselves after cousin Ginger Blake left the group. (In Britain they were called American Spring, to distinguish them from an English group of the same name.)

Also released in 1971 was the Beach Boys' *Surf's Up*, a recording on which Brian had minimal control. While *Surf's Up* included Bruce Johnston's tender "Disney Girls (1957)" and the 1966 Wilson–Parks title track, it also featured a song (that the group objected to) that signaled Brian's precarious mental state: his autobiographical "'Til I Die."

Brian's major contribution to the Beach Boys 1972 *Holland* was "Sail on Sailor," which he'd written with several people, including Van Dyke Parks. Originally rejected by Reprise, who distributed the Beach Boys' records from 1970 to 1979, the album charted at number 36. A year later, fear so dominated Brian's existence that he remained in seclusion, rarely making an appearance wearing anything but pajamas. The death of Murry Wilson in June 1973 hastened another breakdown, causing Brian to flee Los Angeles and the funeral service. The years since Murry's separation from the group hadn't been kind. Although he'd fought voraciously to keep outsiders from penetrating the family business, Murry had vindictively began to manage another surf group (the Sunrays) in 1964, and had begun producing them for Capitol Records. While his protégés enjoyed a modicum of success, they didn't pose any threat to the Beach Boys, who at one time used them as an opening act.

Murry committed his worst atrocity in 1969, however, when he sold the Sea of Tunes catalog—Brian's lifework—to Irvin Almo (the publishing arm of A&M Records) for $700,000. (The songs—worth millions of dollars—have been the focus of numerous lawsuits in recent years. In 1989 Brian sued to reclaim the copyrights, asking for $100 million in back royalties. The suit was settled out of court in 1992, and he received $10 million. After suing Brian in 1994, Mike Love won songwriting credit, $5 million in back royalties, and a share of future royalties on 35 Beach Boys tunes to which he had contributed.)

Brian attributed his decline in the 1970s to Murry's death, explaining that, "My father's dying had a lot to do with my retreating." The stories—many of them dubious—are legendary. What is clear from most accounts is that by the early '70s, Brian Wilson was little more than a stereotypical bum, albeit a rich one. When the family attempted to restrict his access to cash (theorizing that he would otherwise squander it), he took to wandering the streets of Los Angeles begging rides, drugs, and booze. By the time Capitol released *Endless Summer* (a million-selling double album of early hits), Brian couldn't have cared less about the public's perception of him or the Beach Boys.

In late 1975, Marilyn hired Dr. Eugene Landy, a psychologist whose unorthodox and questionable techniques had aided several celebrities including Rod Steiger and Alice Cooper. Working to combat years of self-destructive behavior, Landy orchestrated the "second coming" of Brian Wilson, spearheading the misguided "Brian Is Back" commercial campaign. A comeback album, *15 Big Ones*, compared to earlier efforts, was an artistic failure. Despite its shortcomings it still charted at number 8 on the *Billboard* charts (their best showing since the *Beach Boys Party!* album hit number 6 in 1965).

It wasn't until 1977 and *The Beach Boys Love You* that Brian reemerged, writing, playing, and singing the songs practically by himself. Though far from perfect, the album proved that Brian had retained the capacity to write and produce with the best. While he may have recovered some of his studio prowess, his behavior with the Beach Boys was uneven and embarrassing—both onstage and off. He frequently found himself in conflict with Mike, Carl, or one of the other Beach Boys. Realizing how dysfunctional the family's situation had become, Marilyn left with the children in 1978.

The Landy Years
In November 1982, Brian was fired from the band—a move that the rest of the Beach Boys hoped would save his life. A

lifeline came in 1983 via Eugene Landy. Reintroduced to Brian's life, Landy began smothering his patient, severing his connection with those who loved and cared about him.

Isolating him further was the December 1983 death of Dennis Wilson, who drowned in Marina del Rey. Shortly after Dennis's passing, Brian was diagnosed with paranoid schizophrenia and manic depression. It was clear to the psychologists that his mental opacity was a consequence of prolonged drug use; medical tests indicated that he suffered irreparable brain damage from his years of chemical dependency.

In treating Brian, Landy fostered a pathetic dependency in his client, depriving him of the self-sufficiency and familial support that he desperately required. People close to Brian at the time confirm that Landy's control bordered on the obsessive, and that he had quickly cut Brian's ties with anyone that he perceived was becoming "too attached." When Landy began taking songwriting and producer credit on albums and supervising Brian's financial affairs, Brian's estranged family and other members of the Beach Boys finally interceded. Ultimately, in 1991, a California Superior Court judge severed all personal and professional relations between the doctor and his client.

For all his faults, Eugene Landy had a positive effect on Brian Wilson, and Brian remains pragmatic about their relationship and thankful that Landy helped turn his life around. "I don't regret it. I loved the guy—he saved me," Wilson told Sean O'Hagan in a 2002 interview for London's *The Observer*. "Exercise saved me. There is no drug in the world like it. He pushed me beyond my limits and stopped me being fearful of the world."

The Phoenix

Musically, the Landy years were uneven. Despite the best efforts of the Beach Boys to involve Brian in recording projects, he contributed little to the creative process he'd helped define as a composer and producer 25 years before. If during the *Pet Sounds* era Brian was the durable locomotive powering the train, he was now the caboose, dragged along by the band's decreasing momentum.

By the time the Beach Boys were inducted into the Rock and Roll Hall of Fame in January 1988, Brian had begun work on a Warner Bros./Sire Records solo album with producer Andy Paley. Although his movement was still restricted by Landy, songs such as "Love and Mercy" and "Rio Grande" revealed a glimpse of the old Brian Wilson. Once liberated from Eugene Landy's imposing rule, Brian flourished.

Among Brian's first notable work of the new decade was his 1990 collaboration with Linda Ronstadt on Jimmy Webb's "Adios." Webb marveled at how intact Wilson's musical acumen was, given the difficulties he'd surmounted. "From what I was told, he went in to Skywalker Sound and put on a magic show," the songwriter says. "It was a real *This is how you do a head vocal arrangement* demonstration in which he created all of the parts on the spot, laying down one vocal after another. He was in complete control of the situation, and went right through the process from beginning to end. In my estimation, the results were pretty special. I was very happy, and very proud of that meeting—that chance for a brush with greatness. It was a wonderful thing for me and my song."

Another milestone was the first compact disc release of *Pet Sounds*, which slipped onto record store shelves with little fanfare in 1990. Was it destined to remain the quintessential "musician's album"? While embraced by hard-core fanatics, it was still considered an insider's record—a quasi–cult classic. Though hard to believe today, the album had been treated with reckless abandon in the years since its creation.

Between 1966 and 1996, numerous versions of the album were released. Shortly after the original mono album was put out, Capitol issued a "Duophonic" version, using phasing and equalization to simulate stereo. In 1967 Capitol reissued *Pet Sounds* as part of the *Beach Boys Deluxe Set*, a three-LP box that included *The Beach Boys Today!* and *Summer Days (and Summer Nights!!)*

In 1972 the band's Brother Records label concluded a distribution deal with Warner/Reprise, and *Pet Sounds* was again included on a combination set, this time paired with *Carl and the Passions*. In May 1974, Reprise rereleased *Pet Sounds* as a single album. Oddly, not one *Pet Sounds* track was included on that year's *Endless Summer*, the award-winning Capitol retrospective that gave rise to the band's resurgence. After 1974, *Pet Sounds* faded into obscurity, lying dormant for 16 years until Capitol's 1990 CD issue.

Two years later in 1992, Brian briefly rejoined the Beach Boys, contributing to their *Summer in Paradise* album. He tentatively began rebuilding his life, searching for the substance-free happiness that always seemed to elude him.

A turning point came in 1993, with a request from Van Dyke Parks. Would Brian sing on his new album, *Orange Crate Art*? Brian accepted the challenge, and the dazzling vocals that he arranged for the title track announced to the world that Brian Wilson was back. A well-received documentary film and solo album called *I Just Wasn't Made for These Times* (produced by Don Was) followed, and with them Brian leaped back into the real world.

As 1993 rolled on, Capitol Records issued *Good Vibrations: Thirty Years of the Beach Boys*, a boxed set featuring 141 tunes. Included were demos, outtakes, and unreleased segments of the aborted *Smile* album. Of greatest interest was a bonus disc featuring isolated vocal tracks, instrumental beds, and open mike session recordings for "Good Vibrations" and several songs from *Pet Sounds*.

Brian and Marilyn Wilson's marriage had finally ended in 1979. In the early 1990s, Brian began dating former model Melinda Ledbetter, a woman he'd seen during the Landy period. Landy had sensed that their friendship was close, and he had discouraged Brian from seeing her. Now, Brian and Melinda became reacquainted, and they married on February 6, 1995, in an oceanfront chapel on the tip of Palos Verdes. Their adoption of two girls, Daria and Delanie, has allowed Brian to fully experience fatherhood, a challenge he can better appreciate the second time around.

With his marriage to Melinda, Brian thrived, both creatively and emotionally. "In the fall of 1995, during the time of *Orange Crate Art* and *I Just Wasn't Made for These Times*, a reporter asked him why it seemed he was suddenly so active again," notes David Leaf. "Brian summed it up in four words: 'I have emotional security.' I can sum up who is responsible for his emotional security in two words: Melinda Wilson. Without her, we wouldn't be talking about tours and new records. It's as simple as that."

pet sounds **revisited**

"I'm not a genius—I'm just a hardworking guy."
Brian Wilson

"As an artist, Brian has reclaimed his legacy."
David Leaf

Between 1995 and 2002, Brian Wilson enjoyed a tremendous transformation: a resurrection that heralded his artistic rebirth; a resurrection that has solidified his place in American musical history. More than anything, *Pet Sounds* was responsible for this personal rejuvenation, and for bringing Brian's music to a new generation of listeners. It all began in 1990, with Capitol's first domestic compact disc release of the album.

The Art of Remastering
When digital CD technology was introduced in the mid-1980s, the major record labels scrambled to transfer their analog masters to the new format. In doing so, they often bypassed their better sounding unmixed session tapes in favor of readily available two-track LP assembly masters. While the CDs that were remastered from these sources eliminated the physical anomalies associated with vinyl (ticks, pops, and scratches), the sonic deficiencies of the pre-mixed vintage album masters were magnified.

In preparing the first *Pet Sounds* CD, Capitol producer Mark Linett used the original 1966 mono album master, a tape that had been compressed, equalized, and limited to accommodate the limitations of that era's vinyl technology. In addition, decades of wear and improper storage had caused physical tape damage such as dropouts and electrostatic noise. It was not the best source for high-resolution remastering; in order to minimize the effect of these anomalies on the compact disc, Linett treated the tape with Sonic Solutions "No Noise" processing.

Generally, the best remasters come from first-generation recording elements—the unmixed session reels. "Getting as close as possible to the original recordings makes a big difference in the sound," confirms Linett. "When you listen to the original session tapes of many records from this era, you discover how much better they sound. Bear in mind that the LP master for an album could be several generations removed from the original session tape. For example, 'God Only Knows' was cut on three-track, mixed to mono on one channel of an eight-track tape, and ultimately mixed down to a 15-ips, 1/4-inch tape. That means it was two generations removed from the original before the record was pressed. When you factor in all the wear and tear on the mono master after 40 years, there's an awful lot of sonic deficiency to contend with."

The deficiencies were addressed when Linett and others worked on subsequent digital remasterings of the album. In 1995 DCC issued a gold-plated 20-bit audiophile version of the album, mastered by recording engineer Steve Hoffman. For this issue, Hoffman used a safety copy of Capitol's mono master—a tape one generation removed from the original master. DCC's limited edition 180-gram vinyl LP pressing of the album garnered numerous accolades, and some feel that it comes closest to capturing the spirit and punch of Brian's original 1966 mix.

Michael Fremer, writing in the Fall 1995 issue of *The Tracking Angle* wrote, "This LP beats every other pressing I've heard and Hoffman's own gold CD, good as that is. This record is truly three-dimensional. Otherwise buried details emerge here between the previously compressed physical spaces between instruments. [The] bass is liquid: a string being plucked. High frequency extension is superb: sweet, yet properly bright. And all of the recording's faults are laid bare too: overload distortion, noise, edits, and the rest. But, if you want to hear the master tape of *Pet Sounds* as Brian Wilson intended it to sound, here it is."

Could *Pet Sounds* really sound any better? The answer came in 1997, when Capitol Records released the ultimate *Pet Sounds* anthology: a four-CD collection titled *The Pet Sounds Sessions*. Produced and annotated by Mark Linett, David Leaf, and Brian Wilson, the Grammy-nominated set is packed with instrumental backing tracks, isolated vocals, session recordings, and a plethora of revelatory alternates and outtakes, all of which place the listener in the center of the creative process.

The Pet Sounds Sessions Box

Although *The Pet Sounds Sessions* wasn't the first multi-disc set to study a narrow segment of an artist's career, it is among the very best musical-historical documents in the history of sound recording—and the first to parlay a 36-minute album into a five-hour encyclopedia. "What is unique about the *Pet*

Sounds box is not so much what we did as what Brian Wilson did," Leaf explains. "Because of his uniqueness as an artist, the *Pet Sounds* box was possible. While there are other pop and rock records that could be traced in an interesting way through their sessions, very few reflect the vision of just one person. For example, Stevie Wonder's landmark works, such as *Songs in the Key of Life* and *Innervisions*, were essentially the vision of just one person. As with these records, the magnitude of the achievement on *Pet Sounds* is amplified, because Brian was the composer, arranger, and producer, as well as the main vocalist and most prominent background vocalist. Because the initial creation was so much the work of one individual, the opportunity to explore it from the inside out is also unparalleled, and Brian's allowing us to do it with *Pet Sounds* was a tremendous privilege for Mark and I."

In addition to the rarities, the boxed set includes two complete versions of the album: the original mono mix and a first-time stereo mix, which was created by Linett and Brian Wilson. The bold move stimulated discussion, and music buffs and audiophiles traded opinions regarding the ethics of tampering with recording history.

Does the stereo mix shed new light on the original recordings and unveil nuances that were formerly buried in the deepest recesses of the record, or does it corrupt the power and integrity of Brian's thoughtfully balanced monophonic mix? Is it an extension of Brian's art, or is it revisionism? "With the stereo mix, you'll hear *Pet Sounds* in a completely new way," Leaf explains. "Not better, not definitive—just different. Some will find it preferable to Brian's original mono master; others will dismiss it as tampering with perfection. It should be noted, however, that it is not presented as a 'superior' version of Brian's master-work, but as an educational, interesting, entertaining, and fresh way of listening to the album."

Although purists may disagree, there are merits to hearing *Pet Sounds* in stereo. In a *Stereophile* interview, producer Don Was praised the stereo remix. "I just had a real lesson," he explained. "I heard these new stereo mixes of *Pet Sounds*. It's pretty fucking good. I don't think that the feel is altered substantially, and yet I'm hearing stuff that I never knew was in there. That's always been the Holy Grail of mono rock 'n' roll. And, it's fine in stereo."

To this writer, who grew up on (and still adores) the mono record, the stereo mix is a revelation. Though the purist in me momentarily grappled with the propriety of altering such a prized original, I was knocked out by the spaciousness of Linett's fine stereo mix, and welcomed the detail that it brought to the fore. The stereo mix is no gimmick—it is a crisp, clean mix that liberates previously isolated elements, allowing us to hear Brian's musical and technical experimen-tation with unprecedented clarity.

It is important for the historian or music buff seeking to analyze how Brian worked as a composer, arranger, and producer to zero in on the finest of nuances. Historically speaking, while the stereo mix cannot supplant the mono, it is an invaluable resource for those who revere the original 36-minute album, and a fabulous way to enjoy the beautiful instru-mental and vocal layering that Brian conscientiously achieved.

Since Linett was able to utilize the first-generation session recordings, the stereo mix brings us several generations closer to what Brian Wilson and his colleagues heard in the studio. As he explains, Linett used the original mono mix as a guide. "In mixing *Pet Sounds* in stereo, I tried to stay as close as possible to the original balances. It wasn't that difficult to do—there are only 10 or 11 tracks in most cases. I remember a few instances, like on 'That's Not Me,' where Brian asked me to remix it because he thought the 'clack' in the bridge was too loud. On most of the tracks, a lot of the balance is what Brian created anyway—there really isn't a whole lot of choice. The fewer tracks you have to choose from, the easier it is."

In addition to making adjustments that suited Brian Wilson, returning to the original tapes allowed Linett to "clean up" some of the sloppiness inherent in the original mono mix. As he recalls, creating the stereo mix offered the chance to minimize the anomalies—even if it did cause some minor problems: "The abrupt edit on 'Wouldn't It Be Nice' was an edit that took an older mix with Mike Love singing and put it in the bridge. I didn't figure that out for years! Because it was a single, the mono mix for the song was on a Capitol 'phonoreel'—a spool of tape they used to archive singles. They had this odd procedure where they would take the original recording of a single off the album master, splice it onto a phonoreel, and then put a copy back onto the album reel. In the case of 'Wouldn't It Be Nice,' no one noted the number of the phonoreel they put it on. So, somewhere at Capitol is the original mixdown of 'Wouldn't It Be Nice.'

"When I did the stereo remix, I was able to clean up the edit—but since we didn't have an isolated track of Mike Love singing the bridge, I had to use Brian's vocal. In the time since the boxed set came out, I've been able to correct that, and restore Mike's vocal to the bridge on the stereo version. But I still hear the stereo version of the song on the radio, with Brian's vocal! Now, even if you like the way Brian sounds in the bridge, that's not how the record was made. The problem is, three-quarters of the world doesn't realize it."

Until the release of the exhaustive *The Pet Sounds Sessions* boxed set, such minutiae—seemingly inconsequential quirks and facts such as which vocal bridge was used on "Wouldn't It Be Nice," and the absence, presence, or loudness of the percussive effects on "That's Not Me"—were details that only a hardcore Beach Boys fanatic would know, or appreciate. The rediscovery of *Pet Sounds*, and the hubbub surrounding the boxed set, helped to change our perception, not only of the album, but also of the way that art intertwines with technology during the creative process.

The meticulous work reflected in the *Pet Sounds* boxed set and the dedication of professionals such as David Leaf and Mark Linett has helped to create an unprecedented awareness in Brian Wilson's music, and has pushed *Pet Sounds* to the forefront of our musical consciousness.

For Leaf, the relationship with Brian is both personal and professional; he and his wife Eva are among the artist's closest confidantes. In 1978 Leaf wrote the first serious study of Brian's music, *The Beach Boys and the California Myth*. He continues to write extensively on the subject, annotating and co-producing nearly every one of Brian's and the Beach Boys' CD reissues. Apart from Melinda Wilson, Leaf remains Brian's most ardent supporter, championing his friend's amazing renaissance at every turn.

As well as having co-produced and annotated the *Pet Sounds* boxed set, Linett (who first worked with Brian as the main engineer on his 1988 album *Brian Wilson*) has produced and engineered the reissues of the entire Beach Boys Capitol Records catalog for CD, as well as their acclaimed *Good Vibrations* boxed set. He also recorded and mixed Brian's *Live at the Roxy* and *Pet Sounds Live* albums, and recently completed an eagerly anticipated 5.1 surround mix of *Pet Sounds* scheduled for issue by EMI in late 2003. "It's gratifying to be a part of it all in some way—to try and promote the legacy," Linett explains. "I think we've done that—we're helping to get this music out to a new generation. The response of younger people to *Pet Sounds* is amazing: I see people who weren't even born when the album was created discovering it, and realizing how important it is."

Leaf recently discussed his role in preserving *Pet Sounds* and the rest of Brian's music. "Many years ago I felt compelled to write a book that told the story of Brian's artistic journey," he explains. "I continue to feel a tremendous sense of responsibility to work tirelessly to make certain that his entire body of work is properly presented to the world at large.

"At every step, I try to ensure that his precious artistic legacy is released in a respectful way that simultaneously enhances our appreciation of his work and does it in a way that satisfies him. I feel that my two most meaningful professional achievements are *The Pet Sounds Sessions* and *An All-Star Tribute to Brian Wilson*, one an audio document, the other a historic video. In both cases, I think we've reminded the world of Brian's ongoing and eternal importance. To have the privilege of helping get the message out—to organize and archive his art in what I hope is an educational, entertaining, and enlightening way—well, that's a responsibility I don't take lightly. It is one of the great joys of my life."

brian is back

"I'll never surpass **Pet Sounds.**"

Brian Wilson

In 1965 Brian Wilson bumped into producer Andrew Loog Oldham in a Hollywood recording studio. "I first met Wilson in late 1965 at RCA Studios on Ivar, off Sunset Boulevard," Oldham explained. "The only words he said that I recall were, 'One day I will write songs that people will pray to.'" It took 30 years for that prophecy to come true—when the release of *The Pet Sounds Sessions* boxed set focused unprecedented attention on the album and Brian's role in producing what musicians and critics took to calling the finest record in the history of rock 'n' roll. Adding to the prestige was Paul McCartney's proclamation of "God Only Knows" as "the greatest song ever written."

Encouraged by the support of family and friends, Brian entered the studio in 1998 to record *Imagination*—his first solo album in 10 years. The record's tone is fun, yet reflective. Two songs are Beach Boys covers ("Keep an Eye on Summer" and "Let Him Run Wild"); another is dedicated to brother Carl ("Lay Down Burden"). Although they'd grown apart in later years, Carl's death in February 1998 from lung cancer left Brian shaken. "The world has lost a beautiful voice, and one of the most spiritual people I've ever known," he said.

On the uplifting opening track, "Your Imagination," Brian gives a wistful nod to the *Pet Sounds* days, singing "I miss the way that I used to call the shots around here." With "Your

Imagination," he *was* calling the shots: he overdubbed all of the vocals himself, a clear indication that he was still able to meet his musical measure. What's more, the *Imagination* album became the impetus for an extended tour—something Brian hadn't considered in years.

The *Imagination* tour proved that, despite the lost years and personal setbacks, Brian remained a potent musical force. More important, the rock world—and its greatest icons and newcomers—bowed to the potency of his music. From the Beacon in New York to the Hollywood Bowl in L.A., audiences marveled at the power of his new backup band, which featured former Beach Boys guitarist Jeffrey Foskett, and members of the Los Angeles group the Wondermints. Foskett joined the Beach Boys in 1981 as a sub for Carl Wilson. He spent ten years with the band, and began to play on Brian's solo records. In the late 1990s, he would often join Wilson on stage, and also became his music director.

Brian first heard the Wondermints in a Hollywood night-club. "I asked them if they'd like to be in my backup band and they said, 'Yeah, we'd love to,'" he explained. "If I had Wondermints in 1967, I'd have taken *Smile* out on the road. They love my music, and they knew it all by heart. They make me sound good." Founding members Darian Sahanaja (keyboards, vocals) and Nick Walusko (guitars, vocals) began working together in 1984, and drummer Mike d'Amico joined a short time later. Their first album (*Wonderful World of the Wondermints*) was released in 1996, and they received international attention as a result of Wilson's well-deserved blessing.

Working with the band renewed Brian's confidence, and his triumphant reemergence climaxed on April 7 and 8, 2000, with an appearance before a frenzied, star-laden audience at the Roxy Theatre in Hollywood. This historic return to the Sunset Strip of Brian's youth was marked by two highlights: Capitol Records' presentation of a platinum record award for *Pet Sounds* (long overdue, owing to the convoluted application process), and the taping of his first live solo album. In addition to the expected selections, *Live at the Roxy Theatre* featured "Lay Down Burden," "Love and Mercy," and Brian's all-time favorite song, "Be My Baby." Also included was a smattering of *Pet Sounds* tunes. The richness of the contemporary interpretations lingered, making his audience wish that Brian would perform the *entire* album there and then.

The *Roxy* concerts played a crucial role in positioning Brian for a full-scale reemergence on the concert scene, and *Live at the Roxy Theater*, the album recording the event, vibrates with the energy and excitement shared by the artist and his adoring audience. The band was tight, and the show was packed with a diverse tapestry of seminal rock 'n' roll music. Audiences, critics, and band members were all delighted by the robust musicality and high levels of energy that marked Brian's triumphant comeback. "Everyone involved in the tour is thrilled at the response," explained Jeffrey Foskett. "On stage it is fantastic to see such enthusiasm in the audience."

Remarkably, Brian settled into the concert arena with surprising ease. "My wife and my manager and I had a meeting one day, and they suggested that I try this out to see if it felt good," he told Gary Beets of the *Austin Chronicle* in July 2000. "We tried it, and so far it's been great. I feel much more comfortable on stage now. I have a good band behind me. It's a much better band than the Beach Boys were."

With the 35th anniversary of *Pet Sounds* approaching in 2001, Brian decided to showcase his heralded creation. What had begun as an extended segment of his amphitheater appearances grew to a full-scale concert performance of the *Pet Sounds* album.

The Pet Sounds Symphony Tour

While the Wondermints' versions of the *Pet Sounds* songs were remarkable, Brian knew that any recreation of the album would have to exceed his audience's expectations. To guarantee this, he employed a 55-piece orchestra, including players to cover the specialty instruments, such as the bass harmonica, Electro-Theremin, and exotic percussion that had been used for the album.

For these shows, a lush overture featuring Beach Boys standards and *Pet Sounds* songs was arranged by Van Dyke Parks. "We thought we'd go all the way," Brian said. "The orchestra gives it depth, and makes it happier and sweeter."

Addressing the music that reflected a bittersweet time in Brian's life struck deep emotional chords in the artist. "[Playing the songs live] brings back the memories—almost all the way back to when I first made them," Wilson told Jay Lustig in a September 2000 Newark, New Jersey *Star-Ledger* profile. "When I sing 'God Only Knows,' it brings back my brother Carl's memory, since he sang on the record. That's a tough one."

The prospect of hearing *Pet Sounds* performed by a large ensemble was intriguing, and Brian's lengthy absence from the concert stage guaranteed brisk ticket sales. For this writer, witnessing him perform *Pet Sounds* on September 10, 2000, in

Holmdel, New Jersey, was thrilling. His participation was limited (he left much of the harmonizing to Jeffrey Foskett and the backup vocalists, and he rarely touched the keyboard in front of him), but Brian's presence created detectable warmth in the theater. Saving his voice during most of the show, he pulled out the stops when it mattered most, reaching high to give us the familiar Wilson tones at crucial points, including the out-chorus of "God Only Knows," as well as his solo effort, "Caroline No."

As the concert unfolded, it was difficult *not* to stare in awe and mentally compare the aging legend on stage to the 23-year-old whose brain, ears, and hands had created *Pet Sounds*. The power and luxuriance of the music was moving, and as I squeezed my nine-year-old daughter's hand, I hoped that she'd remember this rare moment for a very long time.

Across the US, thousands of fans shared the experience. Although almost every review mentioned Wilson's trancelike appearance and the shallow (and often puzzling) answers he gave to interviewers, the critics seemed pleased, and their reviews reflected the high esteem in which they held the artist and his music. Most people, including his collaborator Tony Asher, marveled at Brian's courage and ability to shoulder the pressure of such a massive undertaking. Between the *Sessions* box and two-year concert tour, Brian Wilson—and *Pet Sounds*—was back bigger than ever.

Brian Wilson Presents Pet Sounds Live: The Album

January 27, 2002, marked the first of Brian's two appearances that year in England. Each trumpeted extraordinary moments for Brian Wilson and his *Pet Sounds* legacy.

First, over three consecutive nights in January, he appeared at London's Royal Festival Hall, recreating the complete *Pet Sounds* album and rekindling a long-standing affair with the admirers who'd affectionately embraced his masterpiece some 36 years before. Then, on June 3, he played a command performance, singing before Queen Elizabeth II at her Golden Jubilee concert at Buckingham Palace.

Although time and years of abuse had frayed Wilson's instrument, the January concerts—attended by such aficionados as Elvis Costello, Roger Daltrey, and Eric Clapton—were met with enthusiasm. "The key to the live performance is that not only is the band note-perfect, but their playing and singing is 'heart perfect,'" wrote Sylvie Simmons in *Mojo* magazine. Thirty-six years and a continent removed from its origin, *Pet Sounds* was alive again, and its creator was enjoying the most celebrated moment of his life.

"I don't know that I could have imagined in my wildest dreams that Brian would not only go on tour, but embrace it and enjoy it," says David Leaf. "Or that, in addition to performing *Pet Sounds*, he'd be doing a half-dozen songs from his *Smile*-era compositions—and doing them in a way that is exciting and completely satisfying." The press concurred, and scrambled for superlatives to describe the indescribable:

"Nobody who was there emerged unelated."—The *Daily Express*

"The effect is stunning, humbling . . . 'God Only Knows' is performed perfectly—plaintively, heartbreakingly, like a giant teardrop splashing over the crowd."—Barbara Ellen, *The Guardian Unlimited*

" . . . Wilson was a captivating presence . . . the band was immaculate, the harmonies perfect. Rarely have I been at a gig where the emotional outpouring of the audience was so overwhelming, so tangible . . . it was fantastic."—Jeremy Novick, The *Daily Express*

"*Seamlessly, exquisitely, movingly . . . superb.*"—Sylvie Simmons, *Mojo* magazine

Caught up in the moment, Roger Daltrey expressed a preference for the concert version of *Pet Sounds*, saying, "Brian on his own gives it a whole new depth of sensitivity."

The London concerts were recorded, and in June 2002 Sanctuary Records released *Brian Wilson Presents* Pet Sounds *Live*, a disc culled from the best of the three shows. The album, a vital documentation that was praised for its energy and surprising faithfulness, was generally well received.

The live album is a welcome addition to the fold: a thoughtfully planned recreation that proffers a fresh view of this thoroughly familiar work. Vocally, the record is impressive: the harmonies are excellent recreations of the original voicings, and although his vocals are ragged and clipped at times, Brian's singing is confident. Anyone who knows the album well will detect instrumental variations, including some unusual key selections and a distinctly modern (and over-embellished) drum sounds.

But let's not kid ourselves: nothing, not even a live performance by the Beach Boys during the era in which *Pet Sounds* was recorded, could compare to the dense beauty of the original album. The new, live album is, in the words of David Leaf, "not better—just different."

But not every reviewer shares these sentiments. Ed Bumgardner, writing in the *Richmond Times-Dispatch*, said, "From a musical vantage, the disc is nearly flawless . . . the problem is Wilson, who is charming in a childlike way, but whose voice is nowhere near capable of the angelic tenor required to sing 'God Only Knows.' At his best, Wilson is a functional singer who must depend on the illusionary powers of nostalgia to pull off each vocal performance."

On the positive side, the *Pet Sounds Live* CD has allowed a much wider audience to bask in the aura of Brian's golden moment. *Pet Sounds* was the apex of his musical existence in 1966, and the concert rendition is a reflection of the new-found confidence he enjoys today. Along with his family and friends, it helped deliver him from the brink of demise.

"When you're walking out and sitting center-stage to perform *Pet Sounds*, you're talking about the Flying Wallendas without a net," says Leaf. "What gives someone the sense that they can do that, particularly when we're talking about someone who was never a 'happy' performer? What makes him want to do it? It's the confidence from the people in his life who love him, whether he does it or not. What has happened to Brian in the last three years is miraculous, and I'm very happy for him."

His survival and the transformation of his darkest fall into a seemingly endless summer have amazed everyone who knows Brian Wilson. "There's a paradoxical quality to Brian, an impression of great vulnerability—a *fragility*," says Jimmy Webb. "And yet, he's capable of turning in these amazing performances, seemingly at the drop of a hat. If he wants to do it, and if he's inspired to do it, he's still capable of doing it."

epilogue

Although it was underappreciated in its time, *Pet Sounds* has finally received recognition for its overwhelming excellence and its importance in the realm of American pop music. What was once an album relegated to the cutout bins now tops many people's list of the greatest records of all time and stimulates lengthy discussions about its musicianship and production. During the last 10 years, *Pet Sounds* has emerged from its out-of-print status, being reincarnated on CD and LP, in mono and stereo, and on a boxed set, all allowing for fascinating topographic views. And there's no end in sight: in late 2003 Capitol Records plans to release a 5.1 DVD-Audio remix of the album, bringing yet another dimension to this nearly lost classic. "It's ironic," says Mark Linett, "that *Pet Sounds* was conceived as a mono record, has gone from mono to stereo, and now to 5.1 surround sound DVD-Audio mix."

Few artistic endeavors affect us in the way that *Pet Sounds* has, and fewer still have had as deep an effect on the landscape of pop music. From its conception to its final mixing, *Pet Sounds* signaled a change in the way that Brian Wilson and his contemporaries approached the writing and production of music. "I felt the production was a masterpiece," Brian said in 1976. "*Pet Sounds* was an offshoot of the Phil Spector production technique. I'm proud of it for that reason, in that we were able to produce tracks that had a monumental sound to them. It wasn't really a *song* concept album, or *lyrically* a concept album: it was really a *production* concept album."

"*Pet Sounds* represents Brian's peak," says *Rolling Stone* senior editor David Wild. "He may have peaked in ambition after this, but with *Pet Sounds*, he peaked in pure display of talent. It was so good that, after *Pet Sounds*, he was so self-aware that he had to go for something even more ultimate. Maybe that's what drove him crazy—there was nothing more. You *couldn't* beat it—no one else has."

"One of the remarkable things about *Pet Sounds* is that, for the most part, the music on the album could have been composed in the 1860s as opposed to the 1960s, and it would still have a timeless feel to it," believes David Leaf. "Brian's contemporaries—peers like Lennon and McCartney, George Martin, Eric Clapton, Pete Townshend, Joni Mitchell, and Neil Young—responded so strongly to *Pet Sounds* because it was completely untouchable by anyone, as a musical achievement, in the last 40 years of pop music. I think that's what everyone responds to. They know they couldn't have done it."

For Brian, nothing could be more gratifying than the unconditional acceptance of his music and the acknowledgment of his peers. "I like to think that among his contemporaries, Brian is thought of as being head and shoulders above the rest, simply because of what he's accomplished—and in such a short time," says Mark Linett. "It has happened already to some extent, and the glory of what's going on right now is that the audience that looks at him that way is expanding. The tribute show, the records, the tours—it's all creating momentum about him that is very gratifying, and I know he truly appreciates it."

In June 2000 Brian was inducted into the Songwriters Hall of Fame (the award was presented by Paul McCartney), and the latter half of 2002 found him sharing the stage—and his music—with McCartney and Clapton, whose performances with him attest to the esteem in which his peers hold Brian. He's been embraced by the newer groups he has influenced, and has contributed to recent recordings by artists as diverse as Anton Fig, Jimmy Buffett, and Nancy Sinatra.

Then too, contemporary songwriters sit in awe of *Pet Sounds* and its creator, for whom they have immeasurable respect. Elton John recalled listening to the album with songwriting partner Bernie Taupin and crying over its beauty. "Brian Wilson has influenced me more than any other songwriter, whether it's English or American, because of the way he shaped his chords," John said in an interview for the 2001 Radio City Music Hall's *An All-Star Tribute to Brian Wilson*.

"I'd call Brian Wilson an idol of mine," said Matthew Sweet. "I really love very melodic music, and Brian's melodies are the most beautiful, transcendent melodies that exist in rock music. It's a spiritual thing when he writes music. I've always loved songs where a turn in the melody makes you feel something inside, and Brian's songs have the highest percentage of that, I think."

From the beginning, Brian made it clear that his goal in crafting *Pet Sounds* was to make a record with an abundance of love. In 1996 he spoke of the album's emotional pull. "It was a heart and soul album; I worked very, very hard on it. When I was making *Pet Sounds*, I did have a dream about a halo over my head, but people couldn't see it. . . . God was with us the whole time we were doing this record. God was right there with me. I could see—I could feel that feeling in my head. In my brain."

In opening his heart on record, Brian gave the world an album that bears repeated listening—a record that never becomes boring or stale. "I find that you go to *Pet Sounds* to hear songs that haven't become depleted of meaning by becoming radio fodder," says David Wild. "It's actually better that those songs aren't so much a part of the musical wall-paper. I like the fact that it's a song cycle that hasn't been completely bludgeoned into meaninglessness by repetition, in terms of any one song."

That freshness is what made *Pet Sounds* a favorite among the musical cognoscenti from the very beginning, and it is what guarantees that its relevance and popularity will endure. "There's no way I can overemphasize its importance to us, in terms of inspiration and our development," says Jimmy Webb. "*Pet Sounds* gave me more direction. It expressed some very intimate emotions—about getting married, and becoming close and intimate with someone.

"It was a musician's album, it was an engineer's album, and it was a songwriter's album. It opened doors, and pointed the way toward more songs: new songs, different songs. *Pet Sounds* was a magical moment in history."

acknowledgments

As I explained at the outset, my introduction to *Pet Sounds* came in 1977, when I was on the brink of adolescence. Twenty years later, I was reintroduced to the wonders of this then-unsung classic on a late-night stroll through Beverly Hills.

In Los Angeles on music-related business, I had visited Capitol Records early in the day, where I was presented with a complimentary copy of the newly released *The Pet Sounds Sessions* boxed set. Perhaps it was the exhilaration of being in southern California, the relentless insomnia that plagues my life, or the adjustment from Atlantic to Pacific Time that was the culprit. More likely, it was the anticipation of what was inside the long green box laying on the table near my bed that wouldn't allow me to sleep. Armed with my Discman and the *Pet Sounds* anthology, I set out at 2:00 A.M. for a walk through the streets around my hotel. Three hours later I returned, bursting with ideas for a full-fledged book that would document the creation of this essential album. My life hasn't been the same since.

The journey from idea to completion has taken me from coast to coast and put me in touch with most of the surviving men and women who helped Brian Wilson realize his dream. Some have detailed recollections of working on *Pet Sounds*, while others—due to age and a host of other factors—remain hazy about specific dates and occurrences. All, though, shared with me a common sentiment: Brian Wilson was an astonishing musician, and working with him on *Pet Sounds* was a highlight of their professional lives.

I am first and foremost indebted to two very special people: Tony Asher and Carol Kaye. Over the last two years, Tony has shared a generous amount of time with me, discussing music and the way he and Brian Wilson wrote *Pet Sounds*. He is an amazing human being, and I thank him for the heartfelt words that open this book. In addition to being the most prolific bass player in Hollywood during the 1960s and '70s, Carol is a warm, thoughtful person who went "above and beyond" to support my work and help me achieve my goal. Words could not express my appreciation for Tony and Carol's time, patience, and friendship; I hope the depth of my respect and adoration for their talent shines through on these pages.

I am also grateful to David Leaf, whose passion for Brian and his music is without peer. More than anything, it was David's incredible work as the annotator and co-producer of *The Pet Sounds Sessions* boxed set that inspired this book. I hold his thorough *Sessions* treatise—the definitive "word" on Brian's masterwork—in the highest esteem.

I am especially thankful to Brian's recording engineer, producer Mark Linett. Mark has spent fifteen years meticulously researching and restoring the Beach Boys original recording elements at his Your-Place-or-Mine recording studio, and his work as coproducer of *The Pet Sounds Sessions* boxed set—and on dozens of vintage and new recordings—has led us directly into the heart and soul of Brian Wilson and his music. Thanks, Mark, for your talent, and for the kindhearted gift of your time and energy during the creation of this book.

I deeply appreciate the cooperation of Al Jardine, Mike Love, and Bruce Johnston—three of the four surviving members of the original Beach Boys. The first-hand recollections they shared are priceless, and are essential in bringing the band's contribution to *Pet Sounds* into focus.

Brian could not have created *Pet Sounds* without the talent and patience of these musicians, whom I thank for the time and courtesy they afforded me: Hal Blaine, Frank Capp, Jerry Cole, Carl Fortina, Jim Horn, Larry Knechtel, Frank Marocco, Tommy Morgan, Bill Pitman, Don Randi, Lyle Ritz, Alan Robinson, Sid Sharp, Billy Strange, and Dr. Paul Tanner. I speak for all music lovers when I say that each of Brian's trusted musicians—living and deceased—has our greatest respect and admiration.

I am thankful to Brian's friends and colleagues, who regaled me with illuminating stories: Bruce Botnick, Chuck Britz, Kim Fowley, Tony Rivers, Larry Levine, Susan Slamer, Bill Wagner, Jimmy Webb, and Brian's first wife, Marilyn Wilson-Rutherford. Sadly, author and *Billboard* editor-in-chief Timothy White died before we could speak formally of his thoughts on *Pet Sounds;* I am grateful for the warm casual conversations that we had, and for his ubiquitous writings on Brian Wilson and the Beach Boys.

I truly appreciate the thoughtful assistance of producers Phil Ramone and Bob Irwin, who, along with engineers Steve Hoffman and Andreas Meyer, provided invaluable technical insight. Thanks also to engineers Murray McFadden and Joe Sidore and to Dean and Jill Britz, who helped to explain how the late Chuck Britz worked. Chuck's value to Brian is immeasurable, and I found the archival interview generously provided by John Anderson and Maggie Magee of Superior Street Studios essential in defining his role.

Special recognition goes to Four Freshmen founder Ross Barbour, vocal arranger David Wright, and musician Richard Battista, who helped simplify the complexities of vocal harmony, and to violinist Nancy Ciminnisi, who assisted with instrumental analysis. Their willingness to dissect and explain each musical component of the Beach Boys' sound was an invaluable asset, and added immensely to the accuracy of this analysis.

I owe particular thanks to Beach Boys historian Michael Johnson, who gave me complete access to his astonishing collection of Brian Wilson recordings and data. Michael's enthusiasm for the subject is without compare, and he was a prime force in motivating me to undertake this exhaustive study. Likewise, historians John Gwatney, Domenic Priore, and Lou Simon provided a wealth of information that helped place *Pet Sounds* in the proper historical perspective. I also appreciate the input of David Wild, senior editor of *Rolling Stone*, who unselfishly gave me his time and opinions, as well as that of Dr. Michael Gerson, who shed light on the psychological effects of drug abuse.

I deeply appreciate the aid of Linda Corona and Sheila Stafford who assisted with research, as well as that of the friends who helped transcribe dozens of interviews: Cheryl Griffin, Kathy Ratchko, and Carol LeFrancis.

Arranging my interviews with the Beach Boys were mutual friends Frank "Buzz" Adubato, Frank Calabrese, Tony Calandra, Rick Fowler, and Jim Liati, whose gracious efforts made a tremendous difference. Ditto the help of Joe D'Ambrosio (personal assistant to Phil Ramone) and Robin Siegel (for setting up my conversation with Jimmy Webb).

Several trusted associates helped proof the developing manuscript: I am grateful for the musical and technical expertise of Jon Butcher, Amedeo Ciminnisi, Lenie Colacino, Tom Frangione, Craig Janos, Mark Linett, Martin Melucci, Michael Miller, and Scott Stehlgens. Special thanks go to Peter Hoffman, an exceptional editor and friend whose judgment I trust implicitly, and to music journalist Jay Lustig for his welcomed and valuable suggestions. I am similarly indebted to Simon Majumdar (MQ Publications) and editors Yuval Taylor (A Cappella Books), Nicola Birtwisle, and Leanne Bryan (MQ Publications), for their patience in guiding the creation of this book. Special credit goes to copy editor Linda Gray, whose expertise truly made this story sing.

I owe a great deal to my friend and colleague AJ Azzarto for guiding me through the music licensing process, and am grateful to her and Wendy Leshner of UNI Music for helping to clear the *Pet Sounds* lyrics excerpted herein.

Gathering and clearing photos requires detective-like skill, and in this regard I was fortunate to enjoy the expertise of Geoff Gans and picture researcher Claire Gouldstone. I also acknowledge the extraordinary talent and patience of graphic artist Mark London, who generously assisted with photo research and design suggestions.

I have been blessed with the finest family and friends that anyone could ask for, and am thankful for the encouragement and assistance of: Steve and Ruth Albin, Linda and Ray Austin, Michele Baird, Christopher Barling, Kristine Bradley, Greg Brunswick, Gerard and Julia Campanella, Tim Cullen, Michael Erb, Will Friedwald, Steve Gegner, Ken Goldfarb, Joyce Gore, John and Marybeth Granata, Randy Haecker,

Craig Handschuch, Jane Hecht, Drew Hoeke, Peter Howard, Steve Johnston at *Masters by Johnston*, Larry Kreinberg, Mitchell Kreinberg, Eric Kohler, Neil Korf, Shana Levinson, Mark London, Hugh Mahon, Matthew Mendes, Patrick Milligan, John O'Donnell, Chris and Kate Reinhardt, Paul Stefany, Steve Sussmann, and Barbara Wofsy.

Last, my deepest gratitude goes to those friends who selflessly "went the extra mile" to help smooth my path during the months spent writing this volume. I could never repay their kindness and generosity, so I simply say thank you to: AJ and Matt Azzarto, Karen and Russ Barling, Pastor Tim Chicola, Amedeo Ciminnisi, Al and Dorothea Corona, Didier C. Deutsch and Tonye Williams, Michael Feinstein, Adrienne and Guido Granata, Chris Hofstetter, Gordon Jee, Thomas Kosman Sr., Hal Lifson, Karen and Reggie McKenna, Martin Melucci, Kathy and Joe Ratchko, Nancy and Martin Reinfeld, Nancy Sinatra, and Bob Waldman. You are all very special to me, and I thank God daily for your presence in my life and your unfailing support of my work.

Behind every busy person is a devoted family, and I have been blessed with three extraordinary women who share my life, home and passions: Barbara, Kate, and Alex. Thank you for keeping the faith and enduring endless hours listening to *Pet Sounds* recording sessions—I love and appreciate each of you more than words could express.

Brian Wilson's musical legacy epitomizes Albert Einstein's notion that "imagination is more important than knowledge." And so the biggest thanks goes to you, Brian, for giving us *Pet Sounds*—and all the other meaningful music that has immeasurably enriched our lives.

selected bibliography

Interviews

All interviews conducted by Charles L. Granata.

Asher, Tony (July and August 2001; February 2002);
Barbour, Ross (July 2001); Battista, Richard (March 2002);
Blaine, Hal (September 2001, February 2002); Botnick,
Bruce (July 2002); Britz, Chuck (July 2000); Britz, Dean
(August 2000); Capp, Frank (April 2002); Ciminnisi,
Amedeo (February, April, and July 2002); Ciminnisi,
Nancy (May 2002); Cole, Jerry (April 2002); Fortina, Carl
(April 2002); Fowley, Kim (June 2002); Gerson, Dr.
Michael (December 2001 and December 2002); Hoffman,
Steve (April 2002); Horn, Jim (April 2002); Irwin, Bob
(January and February 2002); Jardine, Alan (April 2002);
Johnston, Bruce (January 2002); Kaye, Carol
(December1998–January 2003); Knechtel, Larry (April
2002); Leaf, David (January and June 2002); Levine, Larry
(July 2001); Lifson, Hal (August 2001); Linett, Mark
(March 2002–January 2003); Love, Mike (April 2002);
Marocco, Frank (April 2002); McFadden, Murray (October
2001); Miller, Michael (December 2002–January 2003;
Morgan, Tommy (January 2002); Pitman, Bill (April 2002);
Priore, Domenic (January 2002); Ramone, Phil (August
2001); Randi, Don (October 2001); Ritz, Lyle (October
2001, June 2002); Rivers, Tony (June 2002); Robinson,
Alan (January 2002); Rutherford, Marilyn Wilson (August

2001–June 2002); Sharp, Sid (January 2002); Sidore, Joe (April 2001); Strange, Billy (April 2002); Tanner, Dr. Paul (July 2001); Wagner, Bill (July 2001); Webb, Jimmy (March 2002); Wild, David (June 2002); Wright, David (March and April 2002).

Archival Interviews

Britz, Chuck. Videotaped interview conducted by John Anderson and Maggie Magee (1999). Source tape provided by Mark Linett.

Douglas, Steve; Engemann, Karl; McCartney, Paul; Venet, Nik; Wechter, Julius; Wilson, Brian and Wilson, Carl. Interviews conducted by David Leaf (exact dates unknown); appear in *The Making of Pet Sounds* (*The Pet Sounds Sessions*, Capitol Records, 1996).

Books and Articles

Blaine, Hal with David Goggin. *Hal Blaine and the Wrecking Crew*. Emeryville, California: Hal Leonard Publishing Corporation, 1990.

Blair, John. *The Illustrated Discography of Surf Music, 1961–1965*. Ann Arbor Michigan: Popular Culture Ink, 1995.

Buskin, Richard. (Foreword by Brian Wilson). *Inside Tracks: A First-Hand History of Popular Music from the World's Greatest Record Producers and Engineers*. New York: Spike, 1999.

Glinsky, Albert. *Theremin: Ether Music and Espionage*. Chicago: University of Illinois Press, 2000.

Kelly, Michael Bryan. *The Beatle Myth: The British Invasion of American Popular Music, 1956–1969*. Jefferson, North Carolina: McFarland & Company, Inc., 1991.

Lifson, Hal. *Hal Lifson's 1966!: A Personal View of the Coolest Year in Pop Culture History*. Los Angeles: Bonus Books, 2002.

Leaf, David. *The Beach Boys and the California Myth*. Los Angeles: Delilah, 1978.

Lewisohn, Mark. *The Complete Beatles Recording Sessions*. London: The Hamlyn Publishing Group, Ltd., 1988.

Lomax, Alan. *The Folk Songs of North America*. New York: Doubleday, 1962.

Matthew, G. "Sound and Physics." From *The Outline of Knowledge*. New York: J. A. Richards, Inc., 1924.

Miller, Michael. *The Complete Idiot's Guide to Playing Drums*. Indianapolis, Indiana: Alpha Books, 2000.

Piston, Walter. *Harmony*. New York: W. W. Norton & Company, Inc., 1941.

Priore, Domenic. *Look! Listen! Vibrate! Smile!* San Francisco: Last Gasp, 1995.

Ribowsky, Mark. *He's A Rebel: Phil Spector, Rock and Roll's Legendary Producer*. New York: Cooper Square Press, 1989.

Schipper, Henry. *Broken Record: The Inside Story of the Grammy Awards*. New York: Birch Lane Press, 1992.

Webb, Jimmy. *Tunesmith: Inside the Art of Songwriting*. New York: Hyperion, 1999.

White, Timothy. *The Nearest Faraway Place: Brian Wilson, the Beach Boys, and the Southern California Experience*. New York: Henry Holt and Company, Inc., 1994.

Vandervoort, Paul. "Barbershop Craft: Barbershoppers Have It!" *The Harmonizer* (September 1954).

Thomas, Andrew. Liner notes for *Caroline Now! The Music of Brian Wilson and the Beach Boys* Various Artists (Marina, 2000).

Wilson, Brian. Liner notes for *The Pet Sounds Sessions* (Capitol Records, 1996).

index

song credits